Dunhill Library
St Richard's Hospital
Chichester
PO19 6SE
UHSussex.dunhill.library@nhs.net

WHEELS GALORE!

Adaptive Cars, Wheelchairs, and a Vibrant Daily Life with Cerebral Palsy

IAIN M. MACLEOD

Dunhill Library
St Richard's Hospital
Chichester
PO19 6SE
UHSussex.dunhill.library@nhs.net

Wheels Galore! Adaptive Cars, Wheelchairs, and a Vibrant Daily Life with Cerebral Palsy

Copyright © 2020 Iain M. MacLeod

Paperback ISBN 9781946824707
Hardcover ISBN 9781946824714
Ebook ISBN 9781946824721
Audiobook ISBN 9781946824738
Library of Congress Number: 2020903344

Published in the United States of America
INDIEGO PUBLISHING LLC
www.indiegopublishing.com

Publisher's Cataloging-in-Publication Data:

Names: MacLeod, Iain M., 1963-, author.
Title: Wheels galore! / Iain M. MacLeod.
Description: [Longwood, FL] : INDIEGO PUBLISHING, 2020. | Summary: Presents the author's life from childhood to the present, a life not defined by Cerebral Palsy, which he has had since age three. He hopes to inspire children and adults of any age to rise above the perceived limitations of disability and live life their way, to the fullest.
Identifiers: LCCN 2020903344 | ISBN 9781946824714 (hardcover) | ISBN 9781946824707 (pbk.) | ISBN 9781946824721 (ebook) | ISBN 9781946824738 (audiobook)
Subjects: LCSH: MacLeod, Iain M.¬−1963 -. | People with disabilities−Great Britain−Biography. | People with disabilities−Scotland−Personal narratives. | Scotland−Biography. | BISAC: BIOGRAPHY & AUTOBIOGRAPHY / People with Disabilities. | BIOGRAPHY & AUTOBIOGRAPHY / Personal Memoirs.
Classification: LCC PR6113.A254 W4 2020 (print) | LCC PR6113.A25 W4 (ebook) | DDC 920.M33W--dc23
LC record available at https://lccn.loc.gov/2020903344

PUBLISHING
Our Brilliance . Your Success
WWW.INDIEGOPUBLISHING.COM

*I dedicate this book to my mother for her love
and devotion, and to Yvonne and Joe*

Acknowledgements

I would like to thank my parents for their unending love and devotion over the years. Thank you for having faith in me even though you knew the outcome of my life would not be what you had hoped and planned when I was born. Dad, thank you for all the excellent inventions and adaptions to various pieces of equipment and cars. My sisters Anne and Eileen for being there for me. Beaumont College for shaping my character and a fun two years. Elgin High School for their kindness and for accepting me so graciously. Moray College for planting the seed of my desire for academic studies. The Open University for giving me the chance to achieve my true potential.

I would like to give special acknowledgement to Janet Angelo for her superb editing skills and her friendship.

Tony McGeever for his brilliant narration of the audiobook.

Wheels Galore!
Table of Contents

DISCOVERING
INDEPENDENCE

Chapter 1

Summers at Granny's Cottage

It was the early 1970s, and my mum and sister Eileen and I were making our way to Stornoway for five glorious weeks of summertime at Granny's house during the school holidays.

The waves crashed against the ferry's bow as it sailed across the Minch, a vast body of water, from Ullapool to Stornoway, an island that lies off the West Coast of Scotland.

We usually flew from Inverness to Stornoway on a Viscount plane, usually about a forty-minute flight, but this time we took the car ferry, a three-hour journey across the sixty-mile stretch of water to the island. We typically only made the journey by ferry when Dad was with us, as he had the car.

The ferry was, and still is, a lifeline to the island, and everything is transported by ferry—cars, lorries, and caravans, and there were foot passengers as well! Motorhomes were not all the rage back then as they are today, but I'm sure lots of them pile onto the ferries nowadays.

When you are in a wheelchair, you get special treatment on public transport. People try to help you and make things as comfortable as possible, but there's no getting around it: the whole process is undignified if you use a wheelchair.

You learn to cope with whatever situation you come across, and keep a sense of humour about it. Might as well grin and bear it, and get on with life!

Modern ferries have lifts, which means wheelchair users no longer have to stay in their vehicle. Besides inhaling all that good fresh air, the wind in your face is so wonderful.

The journey by plane was a much more enjoyable experience than a long car trip combined with a ferry crossing. It took about three-quarters of an hour to get to Inverness Airport in our blue Ford Cortina, but when you're a child, it feels like it takes forever. Every child knows the refrain, "Are we there yet?" after a mere ten minutes into the journey!

Something I remember quite vividly as we were driving out of Elgin, heading for Inverness Airport, was a house that had tears painted below two of the windows, and my sister and I would say, "There's the tiny-tears house!"

But even a plane trip, with all its promise of excitement and adventure, was fraught with indignities. When you're in a wheelchair, you're first on the plane and last off. Sounds like privileged treatment, doesn't it? Well, that's not always the case, and most of the time it makes you feel different from everyone else because, let's face it, you are being treated differently. It was a cumbersome ordeal.

First, I was strapped into a narrow metal chair with caster-type wheels at the back. The chair was narrow enough to be wheeled between the center aisle of the airplane cabin. Upon being strapped into the chair, it was tipped back, and I was wheeled to the aircraft.

Sometimes I was lifted onto a van and driven to the aircraft.

At the foot of the staircase, I was lifted by two male employees and wheeled to my seat. I could transfer from the chair to the seat on my own.

When we were finally all onboard the plane and settled in, my mother and sister and I had to wait for the other passengers to board the aircraft, usually five or ten minutes later.

Once everyone was seated, and the flight attendants went through the emergency evacuation procedures, the plane taxied down the runway, and away we went.

I loved the feeling of surging power as a plane powerfully accelerated down the runway before taking off into the sky.

Another thing I loved about planes was the smell when I first went inside them, a combination of recycled cabin air and air drawn in form outside the aircraft—a cocktail of chemicals, but for some inexplicable reason, I loved it!

Ascending into the sky, I could see the toy cars driving to Inverness or making their way further north. It was fun looking at doll houses below and fields with their undistinguishable crops.

Flying west, I could see the miniature landscape below, and I imagined the people going about their daily lives unaware that I was taking in the beauty of their land, their little piece of Scotland, from thousands of feet above them.

After about twenty minutes, I looked down and saw water below. Then, we were over land again, and it was fascinating to see the houses increasing in size as the plane descended to the runway. Moments later the plane came to a jarring, bracing halt near the airport terminal.

The procedure of unloading me from the plane was reversed from boarding the aircraft at Inverness.

Here we go again, I would think with a sigh as I settled in to wait. Instead of being first this time, I would be last. I would have to remain in my seat until all the other passengers disembarked the aircraft.

Two strong male employees would come aboard with a similar chair to that at Inverness Airport, and I'd transfer onto the chair and be carried off the aircraft.

My uncle always met us at Stornoway Airport, and his smiling face was a welcome sight.

After the rigmarole of getting me off the aircraft and collecting the luggage, we piled into my uncle's car and made our way to Granny's house.

Driving out of the town passing all the familiar landmarks, forgotten memories of a bygone age came flooding back.

We passed the baker's, where we would buy Cracken's biscuits, a hard biscuit of about five centimetres round. They were light brown on the outside with white firm dough on the inside. We cut them in half and ate them with butter and homemade rhubarb jam, a delicious treat! Just thinking about it makes my mouth water, and now I'm suddenly craving Cracken's with jam…

The houses of Stornoway were not set in rows, as is typical in a city or town, but were dotted around the crofts.

Nearly all the houses had peat stacks outside. Peats were, and still are to some extent, the only way to heat houses on the Western Islands of Scotland.

Families had their own peat cutting area, and they cut enough peats during the summer months to last throughout the winter months.

It is a tradition to cut the peats and bring them home. During the summer months, almost daily, tractors trundle back and forth with their trailers full of peats. This practice is known as taking home the peats.

This was a big part of rural island culture to such an extent that when members of a family moved away from the island, they returned each year to cut and bring home the peats. It was not uncommon for people who emigrated to America or Canada to return home just for the peat harvest.

My granny's house was in Laxdale up a steep hill, referred to locally as the Cluthan. Laxdale was not a big place, just a few houses dotted around crofts. Crofting is an old land management system in Scotland whereby people were allocated so many acres of land. Most crofters barely managed to eke out an existence, thus the need to cut peats to heat their homes.

My granny's house lay at the end of a long, stony dirt path called the Starran, and at the end of the Staran was a green wire gate. It was a white cottage with a black tarred roof, and was situated in the middle of Granny's croft. It was very much a typical old croft cottage.

My grandfather built it when he and my granny married. The house was old-fashioned compared to modern standards. It was a four-roomed bungalow. Outside the back door stood the manicured peat stack. Granny knew how to build a peat stack!

I will never forget the beautiful aroma of the peat smell in the kitchen. When Granny opened the door of the Raeburn stove, a puff of peaty smoke filled the room.

I can smell it now, an autobiographical smell, a smell that transports you back to a place or moment in time when you first smelt that aroma, and the happy memories of a distant past that will stay with you forever.

The interior layout of the cottage was like most other croft cottages in Laxdale.

Entering through the back door, you went up two narrow steps and entered an elongated room, which was the pantry.

To the left, at the far end of this room, was a small toilet with a bath.

To the right was the kitchen, a square room.

On the far wall stood a cream-coloured Raeburn woodstove with a bucket to the side where the peats were stored. A pulley was suspended on the ceiling for drying clothes. A window was inlayed into the far wall, which looked out on the green gate and the Starran. A table and a chair stood below the window, where I loved to sit and look out for hours, surveying the landscape for visitors or the odd passing car.

The sitting room was situated through the kitchen door, to the right, and up two red-painted steps.

It was a bit of a struggle for me climbing the steps, even though they were only about four centimeters in height. That's a lot when your legs don't work the way you want them to.

I had to lean both my elbow crutches at the corner of the worktop so they wouldn't fall, and hold the surface while I swung my right leg onto the step. With luck I managed to get my foot on the step the first time. More often than not, it took several attempts before my foot landed on the step and I could focus my energy on my other foot.

I was young then and had the agility of youth on my side to master this task of getting my foot onto the step.

The room was also a square but a little larger than the kitchen. On the far wall was a fireplace, and on the hearth stood a bucket of peats.

A fire was lit on cold rainy days. It was lovely when the fire was left to burn out at nights.

Diagonally opposite the fireplace was a door and a short corridor that led to two bedrooms.

Opening the door revealed a small box-like porch that had a red painted floor. The walls were painted a pale blue, or maybe it was light gray. I'm not sure, as it looked different depending on the hour of the day and whether it was sunny or cloudy outside.

On opposite walls there were two small four-paned windows, and on each windowsill stood a potted plant.

The view from the left-hand widow, while looking straight ahead upon opening the porch door, was of the cowshed at the bottom of the croft.

In the far distance was Stornoway Airport. I would watch planes coming in to land and taking off. The right-hand window looked out onto the croft and water well.

Directly in the center of the front of the house was a heavy wooden door painted light gray and secured with a mortice deadlock.

The door rubbed on the red floor while being opened, and the view was spectacular.

Directly in front, in the near distance, was Stornoway harbour. On clear days I would sit on the doorstep and watch boats or the ferry make their way into the harbour.

To the right of my eyeline was Stornoway Castle, an imposing, magnificent building surrounded by trees—the only trees on the island, in fact.

To my left I could see a place called Point where the ferry rounded before making its way into the harbour. Point is a peninsula, and lies four miles east of Stornoway.

Across from the fireplace was a brown sofabed. I frequently sslept there instead of in the bedroom.

Listening through the wall as Mum and Granny spoke Gaelic in the kitchen, or hearing their voices emanating through a gap under the living room door filled me with a deep sense of security, of family, and the solidity of long-held traditions passed down through centuries of ancestors who called this island home.

At night, I would lie in the sofabed looking at the sodium streetlights of Stornoway in the distance.

To the right was the dark yellow light of the pole atop Stornoway Castle, put there to alert airplanes and helicopters of its imposing presence.

I liked lying in the bed watching the changing magenta skyline of Stornoway.

I watched as fishing boats on the horizon gradually came into view as they made their way into the harbour. Sometimes I saw larger ships, oil tankers and cruise liners, as they slowly made their way from one side of the window to the other.

The croft was grassy, which made walking very challenging. The long grass twisted around the shafts of my crutches and made me fall. Although I was young and relatively agile, getting to my feet again was hard work.

This meant that I spent a lot of time inside the house where it was fairly easy to walk on the sturdy wooden floors.

Some days, though, when the weather was perfect, I ventured farther afield to the old cow shed at the bottom of the croft, or to my favourite place, the water well, which was situated about halfway down the croft and had a small gray stone arch covering it. It had the best spring water I had ever tasted, or probably ever will taste.

The water was always cold all year round. On hot summer days the water was so refreshing. We would take enough well water with us to the peats to make tea.

Loch Grinivat, where Granny had her peat-cutting bank, was about a mile and a half from the house.

The tarmac road stopped about a quarter of a mile from Granny's house, and the remaining trek was down a dirt track.

Granny, Mum and my sister took turns pushing my wheelchair, an old grey NHS-issued model with no bells and whistles, but it did the job.

But I must admit, trundling down the dirt track for three-quarters of a mile was not the most comfortable wheelchair experience I've ever had!

I remember setting off from the loch side and walking down the dirt track. It was hard going, and my legs were sore, but I kept walking. I must have been about eight or nine years old.

I was rampaging along, almost at Granny's house, or so I thought, but I had only walked about a quarter of a mile. Dad came along and picked me up in the car. It was near the end of our summer holiday, and he had arrived to take us all back home on the ferry.

The Highlands of Scotland are stunningly beautiful. On sunny days the scenery is some of the best in the world.

There is a downside and a menacing drawback to visiting Scotland in the summer, however:

THE MIDGES!

Midges make their presence felt throughout Scotland, but the midges in Stornoway seem to be a separate species. They are horrible little creatures, tiny flies that bite humans and other animals such as sheep and cattle to suck their blood.

For some inexplicable reason, midges don't bite some people; maybe they don't like the taste of their skin for whatever reason. And then there are people like me who midges attack without mercy.

When I was a child, there were many days and evenings when I could not go outside the house because of the midges. If I did venture out, within seconds the midges were biting me to such an extent that my skin was red with bites.

I have seen big, hard men driven crazy by midges.

It is amazing how such a small fly can cause humans such annoyance and total discomfort.

One day was a beautiful sunny day following weeks of relentless rain—day after day of rain!

It was a gorgeous day, blue sky and no wind. Eileen had gone out to play with friends.

I was so excited at the prospect of going out and having fun. I went out the back door, and within seconds the midges were biting me. I had to retreat indoors to get away from the horrors.

My skin was red and blotchy, and Mum had to cover my head and face with a towel and rub furiously to sooth my itching and misery.

The only nice day in weeks, and I couldn't go out and enjoy the sun.

During bad winters when the ground was blanketed in snow and there was a hard frost for weeks, the midges' breeding grounds (bogs and wet grounds) were frozen, and scientists would say that the midges would be reduced in number the following summer.

Those of us who the midges liked to torment would exclaim "Yes!" at this good news.

The following summer the midges would be back in double their numbers. There is no way to win against the midges. They will always prevail. If ever there is a total wipeout of all civilization on Earth, the midges will survive along with the rats, cockroaches, ants, and mosquitoes. I'm sure of it!

I miss my Stornoway holidays with nostalgic reflection, but I particularly miss the cold sweet water from the well.

Chapter 2

Flu Pandemic: Welcome to the Disabled Club

I was born in Stornoway at Lewis Hospital in 1963, and in 1966, when I was three and a half years old, I contracted Cerebral Palsy (CP) following a severe bout of Asian Influenza during the pandemic of that virus in the mid-1960s.

During that time, Asian Influenza swept across Britain with lightning speed. Certain areas of the country were more severely affected than others.

It is not uncommon for a young child to be diagnosed with Cerebral Palsy as a direct result of severe brain trauma, and an extended high fever can cause such trauma.

Up until then I was able to walk and run, and I spoke unimpaired. I was like every other able-bodied child of that age.

No doubt I was a well-behaved saint!

I caught the influenza virus, but my older sister did not. It had a devastating effect on my body and brain because I was so young.

Mum and Dad were first alerted that something was not quite right with me one day when they noticed that my foot was going under me as I ran down Granny's croft.

It wasn't long after that I became extremely ill, within days or weeks, as they recall.

My health deteriorated, and my parents were worried that I might die. The local Stornoway doctors hadn't seen anything like this before.

My dad grew up in the Southeast of Scotland, in a town called Brechin, and took me to see a doctor friend of his there. The doctor suggested that my parents should take me to see a specialist in Edinburgh. "If Iain were my child," he said, "I'd take him to Edinburgh as soon as possible."

In the mid-1960s, Edinburgh had the reputation of being the centre of medical excellence in Scotland.

As an aside, fifty years later I was studying a virology course with the Open University and discovered why the influenza virus was so devastating. I finally understood why my young body was not able to fight it. It's because a young child has not encountered a lot of viral infections during their short life, so their immune system, which recognises foreign bodies (such as the flu virus) cannot mount a strong immune response against the viral invaders.

The child's immune system is not able to distinguish between viruses that can cause a lot of damage, such as the Asian Influenza virus, and a virus that won't cause a lot of damage, such as a common cold virus. Therefore, it is unable to mount an appropriate immune response.

When a child catches a virulent virus like the Hong Kong Flu, H3N2, their immune system hasn't encountered it before, so it cannot mount a powerful attack against the viral intruder, and the virus multiplies rapidly and causes a lot of damage.

My sister was older than me, so her immune system was more developed than mine was. This explains why I became so ill in a matter of days and weeks, and she did not become ill at all.

Each side of the brain coordinates the opposite side of the body. The virus affected the left side of my brain, and thus the right side of my body has always been weaker than the left side.

The left side of the brain is also involved with speech. Specifically, the two areas of the brain that control speech are Boca's and Wernicke's areas.

I spoke slowly because of my brain damage, and when I was a teenager and young adult, people frequently assumed that I was drunk because my speech was slurred.

Things moved rapidly when I recovered from the influenza virus.

Being diagnosed with Cerebral Palsy meant frequent trips to Edinburgh for regular appointments to see my consultant, Mr Fulford.

My appointments took a full day because one of my parents had to take me down to Edinburgh by train. We left the Elgin train station in the early morning and did not return to the station until 7:00 or 8:00 p.m.—a long day!

An ambulance would meet us at the Waverley train station in Edinburgh and drive us to the clinic where Mr. Fulford was waiting. The ambulance would return several hours later to drive us back to the station.

This was the usual routine, but when I was kept in hospital, which was sometimes the case, Mum or Dad had to return on their own.

I was young at the time, and hospitals were strange and intimidating places. I had my fair share of operations. I was the second person in the world in the mid-1960s to have a certain kind of surgery. The operation involved separating my legs, as my knees were going inwards.

Knock-knees are a common problem with Cerebral Palsy, as a result of the altered muscle pull on the bones.

I do remember my legs being in plaster and being kept separated with two plaster bars that went across my inner legs. One bar was about thigh level and the other bar was knee level. I do not remember how long the plaster was on for, probably weeks.

It must have looked quite comical watching me waddle from side to side as I swung each leg forward in turn, being helped by a physiotherapist.

I thought I was finished with hospitals when I had my last operation in the late 1970s.

How wrong I was! In 2017, I had surgery to remove a blood clot from my leg.

One memory I have of my hospital stays was of a doctor with a moustache who always seemed to take blood from me every time he came into the ward. I'm sure this wasn't the case, but it seemed this way in my perception as a child, and his mustache added to the drama!

Another memory, though it's not too vivid, was going on a day outing in a black taxi. Every year, during spring or summer, Edinburgh's black taxis took children from the Princess Margaret Rose Hospital (PMR), and possibly other hospitals as well, on an outing to Edinburgh Zoo.

I remember being carried into the taxi. I seem to remember getting lemonade, but whether this was from the taxi firm or from the hospital, I don't know. I don't remember anything about the day out to the zoo.

Though I don't remember much about this taxi outing, it was nice of the taxi firm, or taxi firms, to do this.

I do not know whether this taxi tradition continues, taking children for a day out from hospital, adding a bit of colour to their lives! I would guess it doesn't, as the world is a different place to back then, full of rules and regulations.

Still, I am pleased I was part of this taxi tradition as it brings back a happy memory.

I was very ill with influenza when I was first admitted to hospital. I had not been diagnosed with Cerebral Palsy at this point. My first memory of being in hospital was of lying in a bed being fed by my Mum from a white cup with a spout.

The Princess Margaret Rose Orthopedic Hospital (PMR) was situated in a district of Edinburgh called Fairmilehead, which lies south of the city.

When it opened in 1932, it was auspiciously known as the Edinburgh Hospital for Crippled Children. How terminology has changed in the twenty-first century!

I only have sporadic memories of the PMR in those early days, mostly of ward one. It was a large ward with a partition that split the ward in two. On either side of the petition were two rows of beds: a row on each wall. At the end of the ward were two large plate-glass sliding doors that stretched from one side of the ward to the other.

Just beyond the doors, about fifteen to twenty meters, was a grassy expanse of manicured lawn.

On warm summer days, the doors were opened and some of the patients, who were in beds, were wheeled out onto the big patio.

I recall, at least on one occasion, playing archery from my bed. On another occasion, I remember sitting on the grassy lawn with Dad making daisy chains.

Those were the days when plants were taken into the wards each day and taken out at night. During the day, plants take in carbon dioxide and give off oxygen. The process is reversed at night; at night, plants take in oxygen and give off carbon dioxide.

The theory behind this practice was that more oxygen would be in the ward during the day, which might aid recovery. There's a lot of practical wisdom in this old practice, as it is known that plants help to purify the air.

Of course, this practice was discontinued because of staff shortages and health and hygiene regulations, and because some patients might be allergic to certain plants.

My days at PMR were straightforward and uneventful, but I could have done without the operations and the pain I endured afterwards!

Fifty years later, I was at an Open University Summer School in connection with a course I was studying, and got speaking to a woman whose husband was an orthopedic surgeon. It transpired that her husband was going to be considered for Mr Fulford's job, as he had retired by this time and returned to his native South Africa.

It's a small world!

The PMR was closed in 2000 and demolished to make way for houses to be built. Mr. Fulford died several years ago. I will forever be grateful that both were there to help me through those early years of coping with Cerebral Palsy as a child and teen boy.

Chapter 3

Have Tricycle, Will Travel!

A s I described in the previous chapter, a severe bout with the flu in 1967 affected me neurologically, which resulted in my induction into the lifelong disabled club, specifically as someone with Cerebral Palsy, but it did not steal my youthful joy and enthusiasm or stop me from living with gusto like every child wants to do.

From the age of six to seventeen, my childhood was spent in Lhanbryde, a lovely little village in Northeast Scotland. It was a happy childhood full of adventures and nice neighbours who looked out for me.

Memories become clouded and transient with every passing decade, though some things I will always remember vividly and readily.

I was about seven or eight when I joined the village Cub Scouts Group as the first disabled Cub in Lhanbryde, and I felt proud to be a trailblazer in this regard.

One of my most vivid memories about my childhood in Lhanbryde was riding my tricycle around the village. It had three wheels and a light blue frame, and the foot pedals were shaped to fit my feet.

Mum would strap my feet into the pedals, and away I would go cycling around Lhanbryde.

My knees went inwards, so Dad made a metal separator that fitted along the centre of the tricycle to stop my knees from rubbing together as I pedalled. It worked fantastically well.

Such freedom!

Cycling where I wanted and staying in a place for however long I wanted.

Absolutely wonderful!

Being able to decide where I went by myself was priceless, and I relished my independence. I would go out on my tricycle three or four times a week.

It was great as it got me out in the fresh air, but most importantly cycling helped keep my legs supple.

The tricycle was such good exercise and beneficial in other ways, such as meeting and talking to people in the course of daily life.

It was great to have that kind of freedom.

Where I stayed in Lhanbryde was about the middle of the village. One of the routes I enjoyed was cycling up to the school and going around the building a few times. I would go cycling after the school day was over.

The reason I enjoyed starting my journeys there was because to get to it, there was a slight incline, so I had to work to reach the empty school.

After cycling around the school's playground a few times, I would head off down the path to explore the rest of the village.

I had my freedom, and nothing was going to stop me!

At the far side of the village there was a road, not an A-class but a B-class road, with a long, gradual incline. If my legs weren't too tired, I would attempt it.

A couple meters from the brow of the road there was a dirt track. If I felt invincible, I'd cycle along it. It was only a few meters circle before it rejoined the tarmac road. I would dodge the potholes and cycle down the middle of the road.

All the years I cycled along the dirt track I never met anyone.

Looking back on those days and the chances I took when cycling, it all seems quite scary, but I was young, fearless and adventurous.

Another memory I have of my cycling days was of passing my Cycle Proficiency Test. The school did these tests every year, and I wanted mine.

After all, I was cycling as well as others, so I needed to learn how to cycle safely too! I was denied at first, but I didn't give up. I had to be very persuasive for the school to allow me to take the test with all the other children, but why not? I was a child too, and I rode my tricycle more than some of them rode theirs, and I went farther by myself too.

Dad transported my tricycle to school by trailer. He was always great about supporting my ambitions and rigging up whatever I needed to participate fully in life as any "normal" person would do— yes, a bit of sarcasm there!

During the lessons I learned how to alert other road users of my intentions and to perform each maneuver in a safe, controlled way.

I passed the test, because nothing less would do, and by successfully completing the course I became the first wheelchair user in Moray to pass the Cycling Proficiency Test.

Being the first wheelchair user/disabled person to successfully complete things was going to be my trademark of achievements throughout life.

I became a well-known sight as I cycled around the village. I would talk to various people on my travels.

I can't recall if I suffered any major injuries. The tricycle did topple a few times, but there was always a kind person close by to help me right the bike.

No doubt, toppling to the ground was entirely my fault as I whizzed around corners and barreled down hills as fast as my tricycle would go!

Chapter 4

My First Set of Four Wheels

A couple years after my tricycle I got a red battery car, forerunner to the familiar mobility scooters, and it was amazing to have my first set of four wheels, not just three. The battery car was similar in appearance to the Noddy Car in the British children's television programme *Noddy*.

I got the battery car from a local charity set up to buy disabled people battery cars and/or wheelchairs.

A local charity gave a battery car to me and to another disabled boy, but we had to raise the money to purchase the cars. We both attended various fundraising events to make sure we accomplished that goal.

Instead of having foot pedals to control the acceleration or braking, it had a white elongated lever across the middle of the steering column with a grip handle at the end.

The steering column went from side to side: turn the column to the left, and the car turned to the left; turn the column to the right, and the car turned to the right.

The sides were open to allow access to the seat. In fact, the battery car was open to all the elements. Besides this, another downside to the battery car was that my legs didn't get any pedaling exercise as they did when riding my tricycle.

Nevertheless, it was great fun sitting in the battery car and driving around the village. It meant I could venture further afield, and I braved all sorts of weather to do so.

When I say driving, this might conjure up images of zooming around at high speed.

Wrong!

The battery car only went about three or four miles per hour because it was powered by two heavy-duty batteries.

I was told the battery cars could go fifteen or twenty miles between charges, but I never tested this for myself and charged mine regularly.

The turning radius was not good compared to the electric wheelchair I have now, which can turn itself in a tight circle. In the battery car, I had to make sure I had enough room to turn and no people were near. In my exuberance at driving yet impatience with such a clunky vehicle, I didn't want to run anyone down while they were out doing a day's shopping!

I don't have any specific memories of driving about Lhanbryde, but I do have memories of driving the battery car when my family moved to a new house in the early 1980s. My dad had built the house about three miles from Lhanbryde in the country surrounded by farmland and all the sights and smells of farming activities.

I vividly remember driving up to one of the local farms to buy eggs from Helen, the farmer's wife. The farm lay at the top of a steep B-class road. I would buy the eggs, and Helen would make a pot of tea and have already prepared a plate of her delicious home baking. I would devour homemade pancakes, scones and various cakes. All of Helen's home baking was fabulous, but my favourite was chocolate cake.

Helen passed away a few years ago, but these happy memories will stay with me for a lifetime.

Another vivid memory I have of the battery car has to do with my smoking habit back then.

It was the early 1980s, and I had come back home after spending two years at Beaumont College.

I had an addiction to cigarettes.

I used to say to Mum that I was going up to the village for a walk, and asked if she needed anything from the shop. The village was about a mile and a quarter.

I would clip my elbow crutches to the back of the battery car (Dad had attached two clips to the flip-down lid where the charger was housed), climb onto the seat, and away I would go on my travels.

The journey to the village only took about half an hour. I'd park outside the shop, unclip my elbow crutches and walk into the shop.

I always made sure that I had the car key in my pocket, as knowing my luck someone would drive off with it!

The shop's floor was covered with linoleum, one of the worst floor coverings for me on elbow crutches, as my crutches would slide all over the place and make me fall.

To keep this from happening, I placed the rubber ends of the crutches into the right angle where the wall met the floor, and made my way along. But this was tricky when a shop had shelves right up against the walls.

In the shop I'd buy whatever Mum wanted and a packet of ten cigarettes—easier to hide than a pack of twenty!

The journey home took about fifty minutes, and I smoked three fags along the way.

Ah … my nicotine fix!

I gave up smoking thirty years ago after passing my official driving test, but I still look back with a wry smile at those days.

Chapter 5

"Special" School for Special Kids

My dad got a job with the Northeast Water Board, so the family moved to the Northeast of Scotland when I was six years old. That's also when I started school.

This was 1970, and in those days, disabled children, irrespective of their mental ability, had to attend what was blatantly referred to as a 'special school.' I remember trying to decide whether being special was a good thing or a bad thing, but at least it was a good school.

A relatively small school of about thirty pupils, the building was in a rural setting with fields all round growing various crops from potatoes to corn, but mostly winter barley. There were no livestock in the fields, as I recall.

The long part of the school building housed the classrooms, with a large hall and toilets, and the smaller section housed offices and another classroom.

The outside consisted of a field at the back and a tarmac play area. As I recall there was a white shelter and a smaller grassy area at the front. The girls played at the front of the building while the boys played at the back.

There were three classrooms in the main part: junior, intermediate and senior. I do not remember much about the teachers, but I do remember my physiotherapist, Mrs Anderson.

When you are a disabled child you get physiotherapy, if you are lucky. Mrs Anderson visited the school a few days a week to put me through my paces, which kept my legs supple. I used to exclaim dramatically that she was torturing me, and we always had a laugh about it.

Mrs Anderson was a good physiotherapist and such a kind person. When I meet her now, she gives me a row for insisting on calling her Mrs Anderson instead of using her first name.

So, thank you, Ruth, for torturing me!

A memory of school that is still vivid to this day is of walking the hall unaided from side to side and end to end. The caretaker, Mrs Barron, took me out to the hall once or twice a week to practice.

The hall was about 30 x 20 metres and had a beautiful beechwood floor. I can still remember the feeling of nervous anticipation as I gazed down the length of that gleaming wood floor, sizing it up and psyching myself up for what I was about to do.

Then, I would hand my elbow crutches to Mrs Barron and compose myself before walking across the hall.

I would feel myself wanting to fall a few times but would stop to compose myself again before continuing my walk.

If I didn't feel too tired from walking across the hall, I would try for the double. The double was walking across the hall then up the hall as well.

Occasionally I was in a mood that said 'I can walk anywhere' and would walk halfway across the hall and then turn to walk up the hall and even down as well.

Walking up and down a hall might not seem a strenuous thing when you are able-bodied and walking is not a problem, but it felt like running a marathon to me.

In later years, as I recalled this walking exercise, it made me wonder if I might have improved my walking skills had this training continued beyond childhood.

Maybe this walking exercise shows that high-tech facilities are not always necessary, and a more basic approach can work just as well. Mrs Barron was indeed an enlightened and inspired person!

Another memory I have of my school days is of a fellow pupil named Tony who was assigned the task of looking after me.

He would open doors, get my meals and generally make sure I was coping well in the school environment.

Tony and I formed a special friendship, and I would spend a few days with his family on school holidays, which was very kind of them because of the additional care I needed.

In fact, I was at Tony's house in 1977 when Elvis Presley died. A newsflash came on the TV saying, 'The king is dead!'

I still see Tony occasionally and we reminisce about those days. He is a good, kind man, and it is always a pleasure to meet up with him and his family to have a nice chat.

Looking back on the education expectations for 'special' children in the 1970s, I don't think the academic bar was set very high, and as a result, the achievement of the pupils was quite limited.

This is the sad part, in my opinion, for anyone with special needs who grew up in that era, or who faces a similar situation today. Academic prowess wasn't seen as very important, but it is! Every child of every ability should be motivated and challenged to learn whatever they can, to explore their interests, and to achieve without limitations so they can excel to the fullest extent of their ability.

Because of my limited early education, I can state unequivocally that my academic achievements are due to my determination and wanting something more for myself than a simple, basic education.

I am not critical of the teachers who did their best for their students, as we represented a wide range of cognitive abilities. They worked in an old-fashioned environment that limited what they could do as teachers.

All children should be encouraged to achieve their potential. Every child should be encouraged to achieve academically whether they are a child with disabilities or an able-bodied child.

Parents of children who suffer from Cerebral Palsy, or young adults who have the condition, must insist on the best, or at least equal educational opportunities for their child. Parents, be your child's strongest and best advocate! No one will ever love your child more than you do. Be tireless in your pursuit, just as my wonderful parents were.

Everyone has the right to achieve and be whatever they want to be. I am not saying everything will be easy, because I know from lived experience that it won't be.

I am not writing this because it sounds nice or heroic or politically correct, but because I was a child with Cerebral Palsy.

My loving parents encouraged me to strive for academic achievement and in so many other ways, from cycling around the countryside and to the village on my own, to letting me drive, and eventually, to letting me live independently in my own house. They encouraged me to attend holiday camps by myself, which I'll tell you about in the next chapter, a truly memorable experience, and I travelled internationally as well.

Dad made and adapted all sorts of things so that I could be independent, including my tricycle, exercise machines, wheelchairs and various car adaptations.

I realised at a relatively young age that a good education and academic qualifications were key to my future.

In the 1970s, when I was being educated, old-fashioned views of disabled children and the standard of educational achievement they should be "allowed" to attain was not given much thought or importance. Education was entrenched by the so-called professionals who thought they knew best because they read it in one of their outdated books.

When I passed my driving test, I began the process of re-educating myself.

I still have the total determination and passion to fulfil my academic potential and dream. I just applied to study for my PhD with the Open University.

My message to anyone would be to follow your dreams and achieve what you want.

I did it, and you can too!

The path won't be easy, and you won't get opportunities handed to you on a plate (I never did anyway!), and you might have to create your own opportunities, but if you are determined enough, as I was, you will succeed. This is true for everyone, isn't it, able-bodied or not. We make our own luck, as the old saying goes.

For this reason, I have great respect for the Open University: they provide disabled people the opportunity to achieve their true potential in their own accessible environment so that they can compete with the best of the best in just about any field.

My school days were good, and I have happy memories of those years, but it was Beaumont College which would shape my character.

Pushing
the Boundaries

Chapter 6

Beaumont College, Here I Come!

I left school in Lhanbryde in July of 1979, and in September 1980 went down to Lancaster to Beaumont College where I would spend two of the best and most adventurous years of my life. As a rambunctious seventeen-year-old, I was ready to taste some freedom and other libations (when I turned eighteen, of course), and generally have the kind of wild fun that college boys everywhere want to experience. I felt unleashed and ready to rock!

Beaumont was run by The Spastic Society, as they were called back then, but now it's called Capability in Scotland and Scope in England.

Whenever college is mentioned, it suggests a place where various subjects are taught. Beaumont College was not like that. Although Beaumont did provide some academic instruction in subjects such as English and mathematics, the curriculum was mainly focused on preparing students to look after themselves in the course of daily living. We learned how to cook, wash and iron clothes, clean, and other household tasks.

I liked cooking, and though I am no chef, I managed to get by. Clothes washing wasn't a problem.

I didn't like ironing. I recall a friend saying that he liked ironing shirts.

Wrong thing to say. He got nearly half the students' shirts to iron!

There's a dish popular in Scotland called stovies. People make stovies in different ways, but it's essentially meat and potatoes, or tatties, as we say, decorated on top with an oatcake or bannock.

I made stovies for two of the care staff who had never eaten them before.

Learning these skills was of great benefit when I lived in Fochabers by myself some years later.

Beaumont College wasn't very architecturally pleasing with its plain white exterior and rows of windows lined up like soldiers.

Going through the main gate you were greeted by a grassy lawn. Beyond that was the car park. The whole front area and car park was tarmac. On icy mornings it was like a skating rink.

To the right of the main building was a smaller building, which housed a bar, dance floor and social area. It also had an ice hockey table, which my best friend David and I enjoyed playing.

The tuck shop was also housed there. The term shop was slightly misleading, as it was not an actual shop but instead a counter to dish out the confectionaries. Students who had the ability to deal with money and basic mathematics could run the tuck shop, and I worked my fair share of shifts there and enjoyed it.

The College was co-ed, so there were male and female students, with one male dormitory and one female dormitory, as well as single rooms. The ages of the students ranged from seventeen to early twenties.

The male dormitory slept about six or seven. The room was separated in half by a row of lockers with a window at the end, which looked onto the car park.

I assume the female dormitory had basically the same layout, though I never found out whether this was indeed the case!

I spent a lot of time in the dormitory ironing clothes and was a model student.

Aye, right!

Entering the main College building, through the automatic double doors, was the foyer. Various rooms went off from this atrium, such as the reception and different offices.

The principal's office was one of them. I can't recall if I was ever in his office.

If not, it's a wonder!

A long corridor stretched from the reception area to a big lift with concertina grey doors.

To the left of the lift, about six meters or so, was the dining hall.

Before the dining hall, to the right, was an automatic door and roofed outdoor passage which led to a smaller building.

This building was where the lectures were held every day, Monday to Friday, from 9:00 a.m. to 4:00 p.m.

Passageways went off in all directions to various classrooms.

At the end of one of these passageways was a wheelchair lift, which took one wheelchair up to an area called Activities of Daily Living.

This was where we were taught how to cook, wash and iron clothes and do domestic chores.

Another classroom dealt with how to look after money: budget, save and generally look after your financial affairs.

As I recall, English was taught in the library, which was sectioned off to form a classroom.

At first the English teacher thought I was an okay student, but as I became more of a typical college boy, drinking and smoking (I don't drink or smoke now), he wasn't too enamored with me.

Ironically, I'm a published author of two books. If he could see me now, he would know that his teaching efforts were not in vain!

I loved this building where the lectures were held. Undoubtedly, the reason was because it had a fish tank. I would sit for hours looking at the multicoloured fish swimming back and forth. It was so relaxing. Sometimes I went to that building after the evening meal just to watch the fish. It was so quiet after the hustle and bustle of the day with wheelchairs everywhere.

The students at Beaumont College came from different backgrounds and places from across the British Isles, though the majority came from England. There was even a student from Nigeria.

About thirty to forty students attended the College, and though there were ambulant disabled, they were greatly outnumbered by students in wheelchairs.

Beaumont is the only place I have ever been where people in wheelchairs outnumbered the able-bodied.

I remember exploring the building upon arriving at the College with my dad, and one of the Care Staff, who was from London, when we told her that we were from the northernmost part of Scotland, said, "I didn't think there was anywhere north of London!"

Like me, most students were away from their parents for the first time.

I had been away on **PHAB** (physically handicapped and able-bodied) holidays since I was in my early teens, but that was only for a week or two at the most.

Beaumont was the first time I had stayed away from home for a long period of time. I was scared at the prospect of being separated from my parents and looking after myself. I wasn't entirely being left to my own devices, though, as there were Care Staff to ensure I couldn't get into harm's way.

Nevertheless, the prospect of looking after myself was frightening, but I settled into my new environment relatively quickly and got used to the daily routine: up at 7:00-7:30 a.m., breakfast at 8:00 a.m. and lectures from 9:00 a.m. to 4:00 p.m. with coffee and lunch breaks in between.

Things carried on as usual, and then my whole world turned upside down.

Chapter 7

Who Shot JR?

In 1980 Britain was gripped by an American TV series called *Dallas* about an oil-rich family, the Ewings, and the dramas of their day-to-day lives and relationships.

One of the main characters was JR Ewing, the oldest son of the Ewing clan and a nasty piece of work. He was manipulative and ruthless, and his wife Sue Ellen mainly got the wrath of his sharp tongue.

In about May or June of that year, the season finale ended with a real cliffhanger: a hand came from behind a curtain and shot JR.

Everyone spent the entire summer trying to guess who shot JR!

A new series was starting in late September or early October and I couldn't wait to find out.

I went to Beaumont in early September.

I was counting the days until *Dallas* came back on the TV.

To set the stage for this story, keep in mind that I used a combination of elbow crutches and a manual wheelchair for mobility.

On the night the new series was due to start, I went up the lift to the dormitory to get my crutches to walk downstairs to the TV lounge.

I was so excited! Finally, I would find out who shot JR.

The dormitory floor was covered with a marbled grey non-slip linoleum, the operative word here being non-slip.

I was hoisting myself out of my wheelchair and balancing on my crutches when the crutch slipped and flew out from under me, and down I went.

No one was in the dormitory to help me.

My thumb got the full force of the fall when the crutch landed on top of it. It was sore for weeks. My thumb was so painful that I couldn't push myself onto my knees and then push myself into a standing position using my elbow crutches, so I managed to shuffle onto my stomach and make my way back to the dormitory.

I had missed the entire episode of *Dallas*, and I still didn't know who shot JR!

When the College nurse came, she didn't believe me at first, which was understandable, given my penchant for pranks, but she soon realised that I really had fallen.

I was taken by car to Lancaster Accident & Emergency where my hand was X-rayed, which confirmed my thumb was indeed broken.

The doctor said the bone broke differently to conventional thumb breaks (I've no idea what the usual thumb break is!) and that the break was common in American footballers.

Typical! I thought. *I can't even break my thumb like most people do.*

Must've had something to do with how I tumbled forward like a linebacker tackling his opponents on the football field. Yeah, that's me, a real linebacker!

I can't remember who told me who shot JR, whether it was that night, when I returned from the hospital, or the next day. Friends probably told me the next day. The one thing I do remember is being so disappointed that I had waited all summer, and then this happened!

My hand was in plaster for four to six weeks.

I was no stranger to hurting myself but had never broken my thumb before. I could now add broken thumb to the list.

I had no choice but to swallow my pride and accept help from others, mostly from the Care Staff, but students helped me too.

It was so degrading asking for help with things I normally did for myself. I lost my independence, and that hurt, especially because I cherished my freedom to do things for myself.

On the positive side, it meant I couldn't iron!

Having to rely on others did mean I formed new friendships. One such friendship endures to this day.

David and I became good friends. He was ambulant and I was in a wheelchair, so he pushed me wherever I needed to go.

Even after my thumb healed and the plaster was off, David and I were inseparable. My antics and pushing the boundaries got worse.

Poor David!

I got permission to start a weekly video film club. At that time watching films on VHS videos was quite a big thing.

David and I would go down to a local video shop to rent a film and return it the next day after that evening's showing.

The College gave me money to set up the club, and I had to pay it back. I charged students a nominal sum, just enough to pay back the loan.

The first film I showed was *Life of Brian*.

That didn't go down well with the College, I can assure you.

Seems tame by modern standards, but back then attitudes were different.

One of the lecturers gave me a book when I left the College, and inscribed it with these words:

'Thank you for the funniest two years of my life!'

Chapter 8

All in Good Fun

Towards the end of my first year at Beaumont College I was given permission to go on a trip to America.

1981 was the Year of the Disabled, and a group from Moray, Sports for Disabled, went to America for two or three weeks.

About twelve or so people went, and it was a one-to-one ratio, one disabled accompanied by someone able-bodied. My older sister Anne went with me.

I was seventeen at the time, but in a couple months I was going to celebrate my eighteenth birthday. My age was a disadvantage with respect to having an alcoholic beverage as you have to be twenty-one to drink in America. In Britain, eighteen was the legal age to drink, and being an upstanding college student, not a drop of alcohol wetted my lips until I was eighteen. Hard to believe, I know, but it's true!

I remember a few times that I wasn't allowed to accompany the group when they went out socialising, and I was curious to see the inside of an American bar. I'm not sure why, as I had never seen the inside of a British bar. I suppose it was my fascination with all things American at the time.

One of my overriding memories of my American trip is of buying a cowboy hat and cowboy boots to match.

Come on, folks, you can't go to America without buying a ten-gallon hat! No expense spared.

As I recall, there were various hats made from different materials. I didn't want one made from white Hessen with a black band around the rim. No sir, I was going to make a fashion statement with my cowboy hat! It was a light brown crushed velvet.

I was so cool! I was a modern cowboy. Everyone has done the cowboy on a horse thing. No, my horse was an old grey NHS wheelchair.

How cool was I!

Yes sir, Dodge City here I come, on my old grey wheelchair I spin!

I wore my trendsetting cowboy hat everywhere to show everyone how cool I was. I'm sure the real Texas cowboys could spot me a mile away. They must've really envied my authenticity!

I was so cool that I actually felt sorry for others who were not a fashion icon like me. You either have it or you don't, and I definitely had it. Baby, I oozed coolness!

My cowboy boots made a statement about how fashion consciousness I really was. The fact they didn't fit me properly was unimportant. They were brown, calf-length and made of a synthetic material with a hieroglyphic design all around the boots, and of course they had pointed toes.

Over the rolling years, I cannot recall what happened to my amazingly cool cowboy hat and boots, but I remember how proud I was of being a fashion icon.

I do not remember everything on the itinerary, but I do recall snippets of things we did, such as eating buffalo steaks, going on a boat trip and taking a bus trip for some outing or other.

I seem to remember attending an organized activities afternoon and breaking two raw eggs with an old-fashioned musket, which no one had managed to do that afternoon. Back then I enjoyed target shooting and was relatively good at it. I have not picked up a target rifle in years and have no desire to nowadays.

Being flippant, now I can't even lift my own arms!

Although I can't remember much about my American adventures, I am more than certain Anne would have looked after me well and attended to everything I needed. Thanks, Anne! I'm sure I was a very trying kid brother at times!

In my second year, the College bought two houses, one near the College and the other in Morecombe Bay about ten miles away.

Students who were independent and could look after themselves were eligible to stay in either of the two houses.

Those who stayed in a house followed roughly the same routine in that they attended lectures every day, did their own washing and looked after their personal hygiene.

David and I were lucky enough to be chosen to live in the Morecombe House.

If I pushed the boundaries while living at the College, then I *really* pushed them while living in the Morecombe House.

It was an old Victorian house not far from Morecombe shopping center. The house contained three floors with bedrooms and bathrooms on the second and third floors. The second floor was for the male students, and the third floor was for the female students.

I slept in an adapted bedroom on the ground floor with another student. Our bedroom had a specially adapted en suite bathroom.

The ground floor also comprised the main entrance, kitchen and sitting room.

There was a specially constructed ramp leading down to the pavement.

One feature of the house that I particularly liked and found amusing was the downstairs small toilet, which was up two steps. The toilet bowl had designs painted around the outside. Climbing those two steps to do your business felt like ascending a throne. The only time in my life I felt like a king, and it was while sitting on a toilet. Ah well, you take what you can get!

By far the biggest plus, for me anyway, was being eighteen, which meant I was finally of legal age to drink, and the York Hotel was straight up the road—no bend in the road, or any other obstacle, just 100 meters up the road to the nearest pint.

It was probably good for Morecombe residents to see disabled people wandering around their community. Although I'm not too sure what social awareness message they should have taken from seeing a young man in a wheelchair (me) lying upside-down in a ditch, wheels spinning but going nowhere, after a night's carousing!

I settled into the day-to-day routines of the house quickly and bonded well with my fellow housemates. There were fourteen students and two Care Staff in the house.

One of the Care Staff would pile all fourteen of us in a minibus, five days a week, and drive us to the College in time for lectures at 9:00 a.m.

There were many advantages to living away from the College. One real plus was the 'homeliness' of fewer people in the house. There was more comraderie among the students.

As is inevitably the case, in every community where opposite sexes live in proximity, relationships formed, but not for me.

Let's face it, I drank and smoked too much back then, and didn't have time for girlfriends. I haven't smoked for thirty years, and don't drink anymore.

As the months passed, everyone got used to their new environment, and it became second nature to live in one location and be educated in another.

The daily commute from Morecombe to the College became almost ritualistic.

I am sure Morecombe residents got used to seeing people in wheelchairs wandering around their town more frequently than might be the case.

That was the case as far as David and I were concerned. We were always around about the town. The shopkeepers soon got to know us, and we were on first name terms with many of them.

I particularly enjoyed the social aspect of living in Morecombe, especially the occasional house parties and other events both organised and impromptu.

The York Hotel was the 'local,' although there were other drinking establishments that David and I frequented, specifically The Smugglers.

I was a bad influence on David!

We mostly, driven by me, visited the 'local' hostelry of an evening for a social night out two or three times a week, depending on the money situation, which wasn't healthy at the best of times.

Social interaction is good for a person's psyche as they say!

After an evening of merriment and social interaction with Morecombe inhabitants (social bonding at its finest!), we would make our way back to the house.

David would push my wheelchair down the straight tarmac road.

How he managed to bump the wheelchair down the step from the hotel door, goodness knows.

I'm convinced there was something in the 'mineral waters' we were drinking, as it seemed to have affected our grasp of reality and how we viewed our immediate environment.

On the journey back to the house, we would inspect different local landmarks, namely the grassy verges!

I would say in a 'where am I' voice, 'I'm over here, David! The road's turned green!' as we both lay laughing on the grass at the side of the road.

How we got back to the house I haven't a clue.

Being young, we were still firing on all cylinders next morning to go to College—at least two cylinders, but definitely not all eight!

On the odd occasion, the house held a party for the housemates. I'm sure the parties were great fun, but David and I never lasted until the end of any.

Again, the mineral waters seemed to have affected us, and the house's orientation appeared to be spinning!

It was decided that there should be a football match held between the two houses.

There were two wheelchair users in each house, so we were the goalies.

Looking back, it must have appeared quite comical.

The two wheelchair users got out of their chairs and knelt on their knees in front of the goal mouth.

If the ball was kicked at the goal, one would dive to the left and the other would dive to the right to catch the ball.

That was the theory anyway, but whether it worked in practice was another story.

The first game went well, and it was felt that this should be a regular fixture.

Although it wasn't held every week, there might have been a game every month or so.

In one game, Chris and I let in a colossal amount of goals, fifteen or twenty.

We were not the flavour of the month!

We had a lot of fun playing the football matches with lots of laughter, by me anyway. Such fun times and amazing memories that will always stay with me.

Seeing how far I could push the boundaries at the College was also a regular occurrence. One such occasion springs to mind and still brings a smile to my face.

I wanted to be seen going into the one adult bookshop in town, and I got David to bump my wheelchair up the shop's single step so I could go in.

I think we had to visit the shop several times before the desired effect that I was looking for happened.

It worked!

One day, the principal came up to me and said that a friend of his saw a teen boy in a wheelchair go into this shop.

He knew right away it was me!

During my two years at Beaumont I went on a few College trips.

The biggest trip was a two-week adventure to Germany. I think it was to attend a conference or something along those lines.

I cannot remember the details of the trip or the venues we visited. Over the rolling years these details have drifted into the mists of time. Only erratic snippets of memories flow into my consciousness with infrequent transience.

One memory I have is of hosting a 'thank you' party for our German hosts, and I thought I could out drink them.

That didn't happen. They drank me under the table, and I thought I could drink with the best of them!

Another fun memory is of breakfast times.

The table would be full of breads, spreads, German sausage and coffee.

I would eat everything from sausage to slices of bread with different spreads, but my favourite was a chocolate spread and gallons of coffee.

My voracious appetite was met with disgust from some of the other members of the party, who only had coffee and toast, but I didn't care. More for me to enjoy!

A running joke amongst the group was saying 'Good morning' in German, which is 'Guten Morgen.'

A few of the party lived in the Morecombe House, and we would jokingly say, 'Go to Morecombe!'

If any of the German hosts remember a self-opinionated drunken Scot, I would like to thank you for a fantastic time and your warm hospitality.

I only remember one trip organised only for students who lived in the Morecombe House, and that was to go and see Meatloaf in concert.

In the early 1980s, Meatloaf was one of the biggest groups in the world.

It was a big thing to go to a concert in London, probably for the first time for most of us.

It was for me!

We stayed in a Bed & Breakfast for a couple nights while in London. I think the Bed & Breakfast was in Kensington, but I cannot remember.

We were all excited at the prospect of seeing Meatloaf.

We were told not to take cameras, as one of the Care Staff who went with the group said that her boyfriend would bring his camera, and we'd all get a picture of Meatloaf.

She and her boyfriend separated not long after the concert.

I never got my picture of Meatloaf. I have been traumatised for forty years because I didn't get my picture of Meatloaf!

Chapter 9

Freedom of the Open Road

I started to learn to drive while at Beaumont. A British School of Motoring (BSM) instructor came to the College once a week from Bolton. I couldn't really afford the lessons, but I knew that passing my driving test would be the key to my future. Having that sense of freedom and a set of keys would open doors.

I was right!

The car was a white Mini Metro, a popular car back then, with the distinctive BSM cone on the roof to signify that a student driver was at the wheel—fair warning to all other drivers!

The car was automatic with a push/pull hand control system. This hand control is probably the most popular for adapted cars and works by pulling the handle up toward the steering wheel to accelerate the vehicle and down to apply the brake.

My last push/pull hand control had a small switch on top of the handle which was an additional indicator switch. Very useful!

In the various cars I've owned over the years, I had variations of this hand control. They all basically do the same thing: make the car go and stop.

A vehicle can be adapted to suit nearly all disabilities, which allows that person to drive and experience freedom, probably for the first time, as well as being able to go somewhere on their own.

All these adaptations come at a price, which is often beyond the financial capability of most disabled people.

In the long run, however, allowing someone the financial ability to adapt a vehicle to suit their needs might work out a good deal for society because greater independence is good for everyone.

This would lead to a boost in the disabled population's self-confidence and social skills with regards to meeting and talking to people. For example, with the ability to drive, one can attend academic lectures or meetings without the hassle of getting public transport, which generally is not suited for wheelchairs.

I can't drive anymore, and it's one of the main things I miss the most—the freedom of rolling down the open roads of the Scottish Highlands, and the independence that driving brings.

I can't remember how I felt on my first driving lesson, but I imagine I was nervous. Over the months my confidence grew behind the steering wheel, and this self-confidence showed in my driving ability.

As I became better at driving, I knew that I wanted to pay for two lessons, but I couldn't afford it. Paying for one lesson was difficult enough, but paying for a double lesson would really hurt financially.

Mum and Dad helped, which I was grateful for.

Every two or three weeks, I went out on the road with my instructor Don for a double driving lesson.

Sometimes the lessons were consecutive and at other times I had to wait until another person had their lesson before I got my second lesson.

As the weeks passed, I soon got used to driving around the local area and gained valuable experience behind the wheel.

As I drove a longer distance with each lesson, I became more confident and my driving skills were honed.

I smoked in those days, and so did Don.

Often Don would tell me to drive wherever I wanted, as he felt confident with my driving, so I would drive around Lancaster and Morecombe before I pulled into a layby and switched off the car's engine.

"Why are you stopping here?" Don would say.

"I'm going to smoke your fags!" I'd reply, and we'd have a laugh about it and enjoy a smoke together.

My first foray into the world of driving brings back happy and funny memories.

After I passed my driving test, I drove consistently for three decades whenever I had the opportunity. It didn't take much to compel me to get in my beloved specially adapted car to run an errand or just to go to the village to chat with the shopkeepers and sit by the river Spey.

I still remember those early driving experiences with great fondness.

Driving is very important in a disabled person's life. If they have passed a driving test, they have as much right—probably a greater right—to be on the road as anyone else, as they depend on their ability to drive.

Parents of disabled teenagers and young adults should encourage them to drive to boost their self-confidence and to give them more independence, but more importantly, as a way to help them decide their own future.

My parents encouraged me to drive and to pass my driving test, and I will always be grateful to them for allowing me a taste of true freedom that comes from having a set of keys and the ability to go wherever I wanted to go.

My parents helped pay for driving lessons, and my dad adapted each of the cars I owned through the years. He lovingly adapted my first car so I would be able to pass my driving test.

Each step of the way, Mum and Dad were behind me offering me support and encouraging me.

Living to the Hilt

Chapter 10

First Car, Best Car

My two years at Beaumont College were coming to an end, and I had to face whatever the future had in store for me.

One door closes and another door opens!

I would miss my fellow students and all the fun and laughs we had, especially the huge amount of fun times I had while living in the Morecombe House.

I hope the town managed to recover!

One aspect of my two years at Beaumont that I would not miss, however, was the train journeys home every six weeks to visit Mum and Dad.

They would make the journey down to Beaumont by train to pick me up, and we would return home by train.

When you are a wheelchair user, travelling by public transport is a nightmare, in my experience anyway. But once I'm settled into my seat, the journey is usually pleasant.

I like seeing the countryside zooming past outside the window; that aspect of train travel is lovely and relaxing.

But it's the sheer hassle of getting on and off the train that I can do without.

Going to the toilet on a train is a totally different matter. A wheelchair just doesn't fit into the small toilet cubicle!

As an aside, while I was a member of the Moray Access Panel (looking at disabled access and facilities in new and old buildings), I was known as the 'toilet king' because everyone must go to the toilet, and toilets should be accessible to everyone.

If it wasn't for the kindness of the general public assisting me on and off trains, I would still be on a train today circling Britain in an endless loop of misery!

If you are a wheelchair user, you should inform the train company of your travel plans beforehand. They need all the details: the day you're travelling, where you're going to, the place you're leaving from, and any train/platform and train changes so a member of staff can assist you at each step in your journey.

Mum and Dad always informed Scotrail of our travel plans beforehand.

I travelled by train for two years every six weeks, and I can count on one hand the number of times a member of staff assisted me.

So, what was the point of informing Scotrail about my travel plans?

I would get help getting my wheelchair on a train at the start of my journey, and then communications would break down, and that was the last assistance I got until I reached my destination.

Several times I had to journey in the guards' van because there were no wheelchair spaces. The feeling was degrading, and it reinforced the feeling that I was a third-class citizen.

The train companies do not like to admit this practice happened, as it's not good PR, but it did and probably does even now to a certain extent.

I vowed to myself that when I passed my driving test, I would never travel by train again.

I never did! I drove everywhere.

While driving I was in charge and had no access issues to deal with.

All public transport, in my opinion, is not wheelchair friendly.

I was home after two years away at college having fun, but now I had to find my place in the world.

I went to Beaumont a kid and came back an adult!

What will I do now? I thought. I realised that the key to my future lay in my ability to drive.

I had to pass my driving test.

I bought my first car about six months before I passed my driving test, an automatic Blue Mini Clubman.

My dad made my hand controls, and they were bright yellow, easy to see in any weather and at night when the interior of the car was dark.

There were two levers with hand grips facing the steering wheel on the right side. Two steel rods went to the accelerator and brake pedals.

Dad kept the pedals in the car so he could drive it without using the hand controls.

If Dad had the engine out of that car once, he had it out a thousand times. He kept that car in top running condition!

I loved driving my Mini, and the fact that Dad had spent so much time and effort on the car just made it more special.

The big day came for my driving test, and I was ready to face it. There were some dodgy moments when I thought I had messed up so badly that I would fail the test, but I passed! I well remember the excitement mixed with nervous anticipation the first morning I drove the car on my own. I got in the car and sat there for several long moments, taking it all in. That moment was a decision, and I knew it. Part of me wanted to ask an instructor what to do next, just for reassurance, but there was no one in the passenger seat to tell me. It was just me and my car now. It was time to put the key in the ignition, start that baby up and let 'er rip!

Not long after passing my driving test an amusing incident happened, though at the time it didn't seem very funny.

This was to herald an eventful three to four years during which I would keep my Mini Clubman before scrapping it to buy my second car.

One summer evening I was driving on the back road from Lhanbryde to Lossiemouth (approximately fifteen miles) to visit a friend.

It was a nice warm evening and the road was quiet. The part of the road I was driving on was a straight bit.

I was driving along feeling like I was quite the thing when I pulled on the brake handle to slow the car for a turn, and the brakes didn't respond!

The car was careening along without a care in the world, and I had no brakes! I muttered some colorful language to myself that I can't repeat here.

Looking down at the brake pedal, I saw that the pin had come out of the rod that attached it to the pedal. I never panicked whilst driving, so I thought about it for a couple of minutes as the car gradually reduced speed on its own.

This was in the mid-1980s when mobile phones weren't a thing yet. The best you could hope for when you were stuck out in the middle of nowhere was to happen upon a helpful passerby or a phone box.

I was in the Northeast of Scotland far from either of those options, but three things were in my favour: 1) It was a nice, warm evening; 2) It was a straight bit of road; and 3) I wasn't driving fast.

I decided to let the car cruise to a stop.

I never saw another car, but I put on my hazard lights as a precaution.

When the car came to a complete stop on the edge of road, I sat there pondering what to do next.

I know! I thought with smug satisfaction. *I'll flag down a passing car. Brilliant … I'm a genius! That's exactly what I'll do.*

No problem! I congratulated myself.

What a great idea—total brilliance! When it came to brilliant ideas, I was your man.

What I failed to consider, though, was my appearance. It didn't even occur to me how I would look waving at cars passing by.

Leaning out the driver's window I started waving at any car that whizzed by. Only about three or four passed in a span of twenty minutes.

I then decided to get out of the car and wave to improve my chances that a car would stop. Leaning against the driver's door, I continued my exuberant car waving.

Eventually a car stopped, and the friendly driver took me to my friend Steve's house. Steve drove me back to my car about half an hour later.

Upon my return, I found the police in the car. They asked me a few questions to find out what happened.

When I told them, they radioed their station to phone my dad. Dad came and inserted the pin back into the hand control in a matter of minutes, and I drove off to my friend's house in Lossiemouth.

Before I left, the policeman told me how they knew about my abandoned car. He said that a woman came into the station and said, "There's a drunk man out on the road waving at cars!"

That incident still brings a smile to my face some thirty years later. Bet it amused the policemen as well. Looking back, maybe that wasn't the best idea I've ever had!

That was one of many adventures I had with my Mini. I loved driving that car. I've had six cars over twenty-seven years of driving, but my first car was special.

Chapter 11

Floppy Disks and Wobbly Legs

Before passing my driving test, I attended a Day Centre. An incident happened while I was there which still haunts me to this day.

I was asked if I would like to attend a computer course at Moray College one afternoon a week. This was in the early 1980s when desktop computers were becoming popular.

To put things into perspective, the smartphone in your pocket is massively more powerful than computers were back then, even the huge computers that filled whole rooms before desktop computers were invented.

I was getting on well in the computer course and enjoyed learning new technology.

To delete a computer file today is a relatively straightforward process of ticking a box and pressing the delete key, or right-clicking and choosing Delete, or just dragging the file to the Recycle Bin.

Back then things were a little more complicated in that you had to write a short program in the Command Line and type Y for Yes or N for No when asked to confirm whether you wanted to delete the line or file.

Well, I was a computer expert now, as I knew how to delete. No stopping me now with my newfound skill!

In those days data was stored on a 5-1/4 inch floppy disk or a 3-1/2 inch hard disk.

To write a program took a long time.

Chris, the manager of the Day Centre, wrote several programs for the people there to use, and he saved them to a floppy disk.

I was eager to try out my sweet tech skills. After all, I was a computer expert, right? Wrong!

One summer afternoon, I was the only one in the computer room. I had a thought:

Now's the perfect time to try my new skill and show everyone how good at computing I am. What can possibly go wrong?

I decided to delete just one line becauseI knew that I could easily write it again, and no one would be the wiser.

So, I wrote the small program in the Command Line and the delete command instantly appeared.

I typed Y to delete the line, or so I thought anyway.

"Oh, God, no-o-o-o-o! Please, no!" I shouted as I watched all the programs on the entire disk being deleted one by one.

I frantically tried to undo the delete process, but to no avail. It was too late. The disk was wiped clean!

My mind raced through all the possible options, but there was no way round it. I had to confess my terrible, awful deed and accept whatever punishment was dished out.

I psyched myself in readiness.

As it turned out, Chris didn't even raise his voice. Of course he was upset with me, but his punishment was reasonable: I had to rewrite all the programs.

It took several weeks, but I did it, and he was satisfied with the result.

I got off lightly and felt so lucky.

Chris's calmness has stayed with me all these years. He taught me a valuable lesson that I have tried to live by: that going into fits of rage solves nothing except to increase the tension of the situation.

Inadvertently, my punishment helped me enormously in that I gained valuable experience writing computer programs.

Moray College helped me lay the foundation of higher education, which I would eventually expand on at the OU, and I really enjoyed getting to know the people I met there.

A wry smile comes across my face when I think about the many amusing situations I found myself in.

When I arrived at the College, I drove to the entrance where the disabled access was (a rare thing in those days), and got out of my car. If I pulled that off without any mishaps, I gripped the windowsill with my fingertips as I walked along the side of my car to take my wheelchair out of the boot. This walking and gripping for dear life didn't always go according to plan, and I frequently slid down the side panel of my car to the ground.

I nearly always winded myself and spent the next five minutes rolling about on the ground to catch my breath before pushing myself onto my knees and pressing against the car to get into a standing position.

As was usually the case, when I fell, noone was around to help me! And, as sure as fate, I nearly always fell when the ground was wet, icy or snowy, but then this is Scotland, so that's not uncommon.

Each course I took at Moray College added to my educational attainment, but a night class in Creative Writing gave me a lot of pleasure and satisfaction. I enrolled for it because I thought I might enjoy it. A lecturer can be so important to whether you enjoy learning a subject. Our lecturer, Willie, was very good, and his enthusiasm was appealing.

The class taught us how to write prose and poetry. I found I liked writing poetry and was quite good at it. Little did I know that some thirty years later I would be a published author of two books, both of which contain my original poems as well as narrative writing.

Thank you for your great instruction, Willie!

Chapter 12

Welcome to the Real World

I left the Day Centre not long after the floppy disk incident.

It was time to go and do my own thing.

It's always a daunting thought to leave a familiar environment, a secure comfort zone, and be responsible for your own destiny.

I was in my mid-twenties, had passed my driving test, owned my own car, and was full of ambition. I had a desire to get on in life, and this was going to be the next chapter.

I believed education would hold the key to my future, so I set about educating myself to university level.

Back then I had no idea of the level of education I would eventually attain, but I write this as a man who has earned three university degrees: two BSc's in biology (one with Hons), and a MSc degree, and I am currently working toward my PhD—all made possible by the Open University.

I started my journey by enrolling in Adult Basic Education (ABE) at Moray College.

The classes were held in a wooden building (looked pre-war) which was situated in the grounds of a primary school.

A ramp was built for me as there were two steps. I would park the car at the bottom of the ramp and walk to the building using my elbow crutches.

The floors inside were gleaming polished wood, and my elbow crutches were always sliding, and I fell to the floor repeatedly. I would say to people, "I'm from the floor police, and I've come to inspect the floors."

I did a lot of floor inspecting!

I attended ABE two days a week. There were mixed abilities among the students, and some were there just to fill out the day. I was the only one who used elbow crutches and/or a wheelchair.

I learned what I needed to learn and was under no illusion that this would be my only foray into the world of higher education—not at all! It was merely the first step on the ladder before moving on to more challenging courses and greater accomplishments.

A retired English teacher came to teach about six months later. I was getting a bit bored and wanted to learn more. David had me reading books, interpreting them and writing about them. It was wonderful to be able to see progress in my level of education.

While attending ABE, I decided to attend a class, as a mature student, to study English at one of the local secondary schools, Elgin High.

All the staff from the Rector down were very helpful and couldn't do enough for me. I used to park the car at the rear of the building, and one day I pulled into the car park to discover that the school had designated a car space for me! They had painted Iain in my own personalised space!

All the pupils were so kind to me as well. I joined a fifth-year class. Two pupils, Cheryl and Laura, were assigned the job of looking after me while at the school. They pushed me to class and back to my car, when their timetables allowed, and when they couldn't, I found my own way to and from class.

I attended the school for two years to study for my English exams before moving on.

I look back on those days with a lot of happy memories. I hope life has been kind to Cheryl and Laura.

A funny incident happened while I attended Elgin High.

Sometime before, a friend had nominated me to be a PHAB representative (Physically Handicapped and Able-Bodied) for Grampian, as it was called then, but now it's called Moray.

The position was voluntary and entailed going to board meetings in Edinburgh, a 500-mile round trip, four or five times a year as well as visiting the clubs in Buckie and Aberdeen.

PHAB employed a coordinator, Maureen, to cover the Grampian area. I would meet with her every so often to discuss things, usually in Cullen, about twenty-five miles from Elgin.

This day Maureen and I had arranged to meet at her place of work. It just so happened that there was a fancy-dress (costume) event at the school. I wasn't going to dress up, as I was only there occasionally, but Cheryl and Laura insisted I should. As I recall, my sister gave me an old nurse's uniform to wear, as she was doing her training and had a spare one that she no longer wore.

Classes were at various times during the day and that day the class was in the morning.

When I arranged the meeting, I thought the time would fit in with my class, and I would have plenty of time to attend the class and then drive to meet Maureen.

Perfect!

I completely forgot about the fancy-dress theme.

Oops!

That day I drove to school dressed as a nurse and as I was sitting in class listening to the teacher read some poem or other, an awful thought occurred to me:

I wouldn't have time to change before driving to Cullen!

I was in a panic. *What can I do?* I became more anxious as I thought of the worst that could happen. *What if I get stopped by the police? How will I explain being dressed in a nurse's uniform?*

"Well, officer, it's like this …"

The gravity of the situation became horribly more real by the second. I started to sweat.

What have I done? played on a constant loop through my mind.

The class finished, and my two beautiful assistants wheeled me outside and put my wheelchair in the boot of the car.

They said goodbye with cheeky grins on their faces, and took off on my journey to Cullen dressed in a nurse's uniform.

I was praying the police wouldn't stop me.

All the worrying was in vain as I drove to Cullen without a problem and returned home to change into my everyday clothes.

I left the high school after my exams the following year. I have a lot of happy memories of attending the school, and am thankful for their kindness.

Now it was time to move on to the next chapter in my life.

Chapter 13

PHAB Holidays at Monymusk

I was asked to be on the staff for Physically Handicapped and Able-bodied (PHAB) holidays at Monymusk, which turned out to be one of the most enjoyable experiences of my life.

We had regular training weekends to organise the holidays, staffing, activities, meals, and so on. Monymusk was about fifty miles away from me, but I didn't mind the drive. I looked for any opportunity to take off in my car and enjoy the open road. I used to say that my car could find its own way to the Outdoor Centre at Monymusk because I was there so much! I was allowed to park right outside the main door on the grass. The driver's door of my Mini had a dent or two, and I would say it had 'designer dents'!

On cold windy nights while driving to Monymusk for a training weekend, it was warmer outside than inside my Mini. That was even with the heater full on! The Bendix, which allows the engine to start, was always sticking, and I would have to open the bonnet to free it. This was especially tricky because I had to use my elbow crutches to walk around to the bonnet to loosen the thing.

I kept a spanner in the door's pocket for the sole purpose of loosening the Bendix so the car would start. It once stalled in the middle of a roundabout with cars passing while I tried to free the Bendix—another fun experience of smiling apologetically and waving, and hoping I wouldn't be ploughed into by the other cars zooming past!

But alas, I always arrived at the Outdoor Centre in Monymusk in one piece, and got to work. The format for each holiday was roughly the same, although this depended on the number of activities for each week and how much money the volunteer staffing group managed to raise.

The ethos for running the holidays was simple, and that was to give the holidaymakers a holiday to remember.

Most of the holidaymakers came from across Scotland and occasionally from England, and were from a variety of cultural backgrounds. I will always remember one boy's facial expression at seeing real cows for the first time in his life. He spent hours watching them grazing in the field.

The Monymusk PHAB holidays were always a high point of my year, and I looked forward to each summer when they took place.

Preparations usually started in March, and there was a lot to plan. At that early stage we didn't know who the holidaymakers would be or the numbers for each week. The purpose of the initial meeting was to organise the coordinators and staff for each week.

All the months of preparations were worth it just to see the happy faces arriving at camp and all throughout the week. By the time they went home, they'd had all kinds of exciting new experiences, such as swimming and horse riding.

It was fun for the staff members too, and it wasn't all work. One of the staff members, Bernie, rode a powerful motorbike. I would give anything a go if it was on wheels and went fast, so when Bernie asked if I wanted a ride on his motorbike, I said an enthusiastic yes!

I was clad in leathers and a helmet, and even I had to admit that I looked really cool, like a true biker.

He got me on the back of the bike. That was a whole new experience in itself!

My feet were strapped onto the foot pedals, and away we went around the area. He didn't go fast, but it was fast enough for me!

I was glad that I was a car driver. At least there's a metal car between your body and the other crazy drivers out there!

As an aside, now you can buy a motorbike suitable to take a wheelchair. It has the same familiar motorbike steering column, automatic gear change and acceleration and brakes on the hand grips. You drive your wheelchair into the carriage, secure the wheelchair in place, and take off wherever you want to go.

It looks great fun and I would love one, but I don't have the strength in my arms or the dexterity in my hands to operate one.

One year a PHAB group went to France, and I was lucky enough to go. As I recall it was for a fortnight instead of a week.

One day it was unusually humid, for us Scots anyway, and by the afternoon the heat was oppressive. Then it started raining very heavily. I had never experienced such a downpour in my life.

Another memory I have of my French holiday is of going to a reception hosted by some local dignitaries, and enduring a long bus journey to get there. We were all starving by the time we reached the venue.

Upon our arrival, we spied the tables of nibbles and thought that was all the food we would get, so we tucked in and drank several glasses of wine—out of courtesy to our hosts, you understand!

And then, when we had practically stuffed ourselves, two massive room dividers were pulled aside to reveal a long table spread with an array of delicious food, and we enjoyed a beautiful two-course meal. Our French hosts certainly surprised us that day with their kind hospitality.

I have done many amusing things over the years, but one incident above all others still makes me smile after thirty-plus years.

When I was a representative for PHAB Scotland, we had a Sponsored Walk each year, usually around one of the parks in the city of Perth.

It was good fun until the rain started!

The Sponsored Walk always took place on a weekend in April or May.

I would drive to my friend Allan's house in Dundee and attend the walk then drive home the next day.

This routine went on for a few years.

One year another friend, Shon, suggested that the following year all four of us should go as the characters from *The Wizard of Oz*.

"Perfect!" we agreed.

I had a lightweight titanium sports wheelchair at the time. I am not sporty, but the chair made it easier to get into and out of the car.

I loved to do wheelies in my wheelchair, but I seemed to always fall backwards. As an aside, I was involved with a group called Pals. We went to social events like discos, as they were called back then, but now it would be referred to as clubbing. I was always spinning my manual wheelchair around and doing wheelies. Often the wheelie would go wrong and the wheelchair would topple backwards with me in it. I was the life of the party with my feet pointing straight up in the air until someone came along and righted me! I never hurt myself, as I knew how to fall, but my pride was bruised.

Anyway, back to the sponsored walk, Shon made all the costumes and did such an amazing job on them. She even made a footrest for my red shoes.

I was the perfect Dorothy in my blue gingham dress, red lipstick and black wig.

I looked stunning!

Believe that, you can believe anything!

My friends pushed me round and round the park while I belted out, "Somewhere over the rainbow way up high ...!"

It was fine singing that for the first half hour, or so, but after that it got tedious and monotonous, so I would go silent for intervals then spontaneously burst into song, usually as people were passing.

Boy, did I get some funny looks that day! It was great fun though and an amusing memory.

I enjoyed my years helping on the PHAB holidays. I was quite dynamic and kept people's spirits up.

Lots of happy memories!

Chapter 14

Education Is the Key

After saying farewell to Elgin High School, I enrolled to study various courses at Moray College, which is now part of the Highlands and Islands University.

The courses ranged from biology to mathematics, and were held during the day and on certain weeknights. I wanted to get as varied an education as possible because the educational opportunities afforded to me in my younger years had been very limited. I had an insatiable hunger to learn more about anything and everything.

I took a First Aid course three times over nine years. The first course was to become certified. Then, I had to renew my certificate every three years.

It was a sight to behold watching me fall out of my wheelchair to do cardiopulmonary resuscitation (CPR) on a dummy, but in nine years, the only casualty I ever treated was myself!

I was certainly gaining a lot of educational variety in the courses I studied. To be honest, I'm not sure if I've ever used some of my knowledge. For example, I learned calculus and have never found I needed that knowledge.

I was studying a couple of courses at Moray College, but when someone told me about the Open University (OU), I instantly saw the advantage. In 1991 I joined the OU, and thirty years later I am still an OU addict.

Every student had to study at least one foundation course as part of their degree, so I studied the science foundation course titled Voyage of Discovery (S102).

My first tutor-marked assignment was measuring the distance to the moon using a broom handle and plastic discs. I vividly remember propping a wooden broom handle on the back of a chair and placing the black plastic disc at various points along the broom handle's shaft until the moon was obscured by the disc. Then, using a measuring tape, Dad measured from the start of the broom to where the disc was along the shaft. Using some mathematical equations, I was able to calculate the distance to the moon.

The science foundation course covers four of the sciences: biology, physics, chemistry and Earth science.

When I was studying the Earth Science part of the course, the tutor, Helen, asked if I would like to attend the presentation of her project.

I said I would love to go.

She was a geologist and gathered rocks from across the Highlands. As I remember, the stones were set in a circle and inscribed with the names of the locations where they were found.

I think the exhibit was called Touch Stone. Visitors could walk around the circle and touch the different stone textures from various parts of the Scottish Highlands.

I drove to where the event was held, about a two-hour drive, and had a very enjoyable day out. I managed to touch the Stornoway stone, and it was like touching home. Memories of my happy summers at Granny's cottage in Stornoway came flooding back in that moment.

During my time studying at the undergraduate and postgraduate level, my tutors have all been so kind and helpful. However, the tutor who has made a lasting impact on my life is Dr Corinne Kay. Corinne is such a lovely person and so helpful. Corinne is a chemist, and was my tutor when I studied the postgraduate courses Medicinal Chemistry (S807) and Project Module (S810).

Over the years I've done many home experiments, which shows the greatness of the OU in devising such things to do in your home environment.

The OU now has a Visual Online Platform where students meet, chat, attend tutorials and deal with any other OU business. This means I can do everything from the comfort of my home without bothering about transport and access. Online education opens the door for all students, no matter their ability, and removes all barriers to getting an education.

I enjoyed studying the sciences, but decided to study biology in greater depth, particularly human biology and specifically neuroscience: the study of the human brain.

Chapter 15

Mishaps and Misadventures

When I was in my early thirties, I went with a group for a few days' holiday to an outdoor center in the West Coast of Scotland near Oban, a beautiful part of the world. Oban is noted for its seafood, and is known as the Seafood Capital of Scotland.

It is a beautiful scenic place with the Morvern and Ardgour mountains towering above the town, and is protected by the Islands of Kerrera and Isle of Mull.

It was the seat of the Clan MacDougall, and the ruins of Castle Dunollie lie just outside the town.

About eight or ten of us went on the holiday. As I recall, we stayed in a log cabin in a forest.

There was a breakfast bar and a big table that seated about ten or twelve, and the table was situated about a meter from the bar.

I was relatively fit, and felt I could do a lot of things—probably more than I should have!

Walking on elbow crutches meant I fell more often than most people. I would say, "I could fall for Scotland!"

Up until that point in my life, I had split my head open a couple of times and broken my nose more times than I care to remember.

Nothing too major!

That was going to be topped by what happened next. I volunteered to help serve the evening meal.

Bad decision!

I was lifting a hot teapot from the bar to the table when I lost my footing and fell to the floor. While falling I let go of the teapot, and its entire contents spilled on my face.

This all happened in a split second.

As soon as I felt the hot water on my face I started screaming. I was squirming on the floor screaming in agony.

The events of what happened next are hazy, but I do remember being lifted onto a sofa, or maybe a bed, and my soaked sweatshirt was taken off me.

I remember thinking how worried my Mum would be, and I wouldn't allow the staff to phone my parents.

I distinctly remember saying, "I'll sue you if you phone my Mum!"

When you're in a great deal of pain you say anything, whether it's rational or not. No doubt my parents were phoned when I was in hospital.

I don't remember much of how I got to hospital, but I do remember lying in a hospital bed speaking to a doctor and telling him how tired I was. He gave me an injection, and the next thing I remember was waking up the following morning.

It was dark outside when I arrived at the hospital, so I assumed it was quite late at night because it was still daylight when my accident happened.

I was in Oban General Hospital. I don't remember much about the hospital or the interior layout, but I do remember that the nursing staff wouldn't let me see myself in a mirror.

Well, that's all I needed to hear! It was now my challenge to see myself in a mirror.

My opportunity came a couple of days later when I could go to the toilet by myself. I must admit I was quite apprehensive at what I might see. I didn't know what to expect.

The time came when I couldn't put off the viewing any longer.

I peered into the mirror—and then I knew why I hadn't been allowed to have a look at myself.

The left side of my face, which took nearly all the contents of the teapot, was peeling like a snake shedding its skin, a mass of dead skin cells. I looked like a grotesque creature out of a sci-fi movie! The right side of my face wasn't as bad as the left side, but it was also peeling.

I spent a fortnight in hospital before being discharged. I then spent a couple of months recuperating at home.

I will always be indebted to Oban General Hospital for their professionalism and kindness.

Fortunately, my face disfigurement was superficial, and I made a complete recovery.

Nowadays people would never know that I poured a boiling hot teapot over my face. The reason my face isn't scarred is because of the tannin in tea; if it had been boiling hot water, my face would have been scarred for life.

The only scar I have is on my left shoulder, which gets itchy. The carers in the housing complex where I now live often wonder what happened to my shoulder when I ask them to scratch it, and the immense relief I get when the constant itching is relieved.

Ellie is particularly good at scratching my shoulder.

The teapot event wasn't the last mishap in my life, not by a long shot! I eventually topped this painful incident in my early fifties when I became severely disabled following a silly accident, the infamous *10 Seconds That Changed My Life*, which I describe in my first book of the same name.

Life wasn't all about causing myself pain by falling or by other means.

Okay, 98 percent of the time it was!

I was enjoying my newfound freedom in the form of driving my car. I loved driving and exploring new roads I would say to myself, *I wonder where this road leads?* and promptly drive down it to see where it took me.

It was the late 1980s and early 1990s, and I was having the time of my life. I had my own car, I was full of adventure, and I said yes to just about every opportunity that presented itself.

One such opportunity was to join Sports for Disabled. This was right up my alley.

Moray had a small trimaran boat for disabled sailors. Everything could be controlled by the sailor while remaining seated, from the sails to the rudder. A friend, James, and I went to Findhorn Bay where the boat was stored, and took turns going out in the trimaran.

I went out in the boat on my own several times, and the feeling was fantastic! I loved sailing the trimaran. Very uplifting and exhilarating and a great sense of freedom. Being able to do everything by myself added to my total enjoyment.

I was never competitive, so I'd never thought about competing. I just loved sailing wherever I wanted. I loved the feeling of the wind on my face and hearing the waves lapping against the boat.

I wouldn't say I was a good sailor, as I'd forget to tack into the wind and be stranded in the middle of the bay until the wind changed direction.

I sailed the trimaran during the summer months when the weather was fair, but I might not have enjoyed sailing as much during the winter months.

I was a fair-weather sailor!

I do not know what happened to the boat or where it ended up, but I know the great enjoyment and enormous pleasure I had sailing it.

Such fun times and wonderful happy memories.

I got the chance to sail on the training ship STS *Lord Nelson*.

It lets disabled discover what it's like to experience life on-board a vessel and what it was like to be part of a crew.

Everyone, whether you were in a wheelchair or not, had a job to do thus ensuring the smooth running of the ship.

It was a beautiful ship to look at, and when all the sails were up, flapping in the wind, it was a sight to behold.

Absolutely stunning!

All disabled passengers had to be accompanied by an able-bodied companion.

As I recall there were about ten to fifteen booked on the voyage, disabled and their companions. James and I were the disabled passengers, and Ed was my helper.

It was only a short voyage from Glasgow to Belfast. All four of us stayed in Glasgow the night before sailing. The next day we boarded the ship and set sail for Ireland.

There were two or three of a permanent crew, and I seem to remember there was a journalist as one of the passengers. He wasn't a helper, but was there to write an article on the STS *Lord Nelson* for a Scottish newspaper.

Another passenger was a helper for a relative or friend. The reason I remember the man was by something he did, which I had never seen before or since. He was a lawyer, as I recall, and he had wine specially bottled to mark the voyage.

The living accommodation consisted of bunk beds. Your able-bodied helper slept in the upper bunk and you slept in the lower bunk.

Everyone was divided into crews to take turns for the day and night watches.

Getting out of a warm bed to do a watch on a cold, rainy night was a thought!

One night I remember seeing Alisa Craig (known as Paddy's Milestone) in the distance from one side of the ship when I went to bed, and when I got up the following morning, I could view it from the other side of the ship.

It is known as Paddy's Milestone because it lies almost halfway between Belfast and Glasgow.

When I heard the countdown to something they called 'the happy hour' I got excited.

This is more like what I imagined the voyage would be, I thought to myself. *Glasses of wine and bottles of beer. This is the life!*

I couldn't wait for this delightful hour.

As with most things, what you imagine is something more than what it turns out to be, and this was no exception.

In fact, the happy hour was when the ship was cleaned from top to bottom. Everyone was allocated a cleaning task. When the happy hour was over, the ship was gleaming.

Then it was time for the evening meal, but what we really needed after that was a real happy hour with drinks all round!

Anyway, back to the running of the ship: all the disabled passengers were able to experience something of what it was like to crew a magnificent vessel like the STS *Lord Nelson.*

I was able to carry out a few things in the day-to-day running of the ship. However, I really wanted to steer the ship. I asked the captain and he agreed.

That afternoon I steered the ship on my own, but I wasn't allowed total freedom to steer the ship wherever I wanted. Good job!

The captain gave me the steering wheel and showed me how to keep the line horizontal on the compass in front of me, which kept the vessel going in a straight line.

"Keep that line straight and you'll be fine," he said, and disappeared down to the galley.

Ten minutes later, he ran up the steps two at a time, calling out with a raised voice—not shouting, he was too much of a gentleman for that—in a forceful concerned tone.

"What are you doing, man?" he said as he looked directly at me.

The line, which should have been horizontal, was lying ten degrees to the right.

The captain took the wheel and righted my wrong. With a few turns of the wheel the line was horizontal again.

I wasn't allowed to steer the ship anymore!

We managed to reach Belfast.

Friends of Ed's generously agreed to put us up for the night before we flew back to Glasgow the following day. The couple were kind enough to give us a tour of the city and the surrounding countryside.

I got back home the next day and reminisced about my sailing adventure. I will never forget that wonderful experience of being on the STS *Lord Nelson*.

A variety of experiences adds to a person's richness of character, whether they are disabled or able-bodied. My parents never stood in my way or acted like worried, fretful 'helicopter parents.' They always encouraged me to experience different things, and allowed me to live as full a life as possible.

If you're a parent of a disabled child, teenager, or young adult, I encourage you to follow my parents' excellent example. They never let fear hold them back, but more importantly, they didn't let it hold *me* back, and I am so grateful for their example.

Crewing a magnificent vessel like the STS *Lord Nelson* was certainly one of the high points of my life.

Chapter 16

The Best of Human Kindness

D riving has always been a great passion, ever since I passed my driving test and started having fun exploring new roads in my Mini Clubman.

When I bought my second car, I decided that I would go for the Advanced Driving Test.

My second car was a red Astra. That car took some getting used to after my first car. The car's brakes had a reservoir in the boot.

My word, that car could stop!

People who had already passed the Advanced Driving Test took out 'newbies' to get them up to the desired standard. The Advanced Driving Tests were carried out by Class 1 Traffic Police Drivers.

Tom, who sat with me as I was getting ready for my test, was a retired police officer.

I looked forward to our weekly Saturday morning drives. He would take me driving on different types of roads to find out how I would react to various traffic situations.

Living in the Northeast of Scotland, we don't have any motorways or dual carriageways, so I couldn't experience driving on them, though I had driven on those types of roads before with no problem.

I was almost ready for my test.

In a strange way I felt quite sad, as I enjoyed the weekly driving sessions with Tom and learning how to drive in the advanced way.

The most obvious difference between the regular Driving Test and the Advanced Driving Test is the running commentary you must give while driving: what you are seeing, the maneuver you are about to make, what might happen, and what you are going to do to reduce the risks. I didn't find this a problem, as I've never found communicating an issue.

To tell the truth I found this the easy bit!

On the day of my test, I picked up the police examiner from his house, and we set off.

He said I didn't need to give a running commentary; I only needed to announce when I was going to make a left or right turn, and when I approached a roundabout.

I was enjoying the drive, and at one point I commented, "On the right side grass verge, you will see a dead rabbit!" This brought a smile to the examiner's face.

I passed the test, and by that token became the first wheelchair user in Moray to pass the Advanced Driving Test.

Advance Driving won't make you a better driver or give you superpowers or other such skills, but it will give you more confidence as a driver. That's what I found anyway.

I enjoyed my Advanced Driving and am glad I did it as I had many years of fun driving all the different cars I owned.

I loved driving and would often go out driving just for the sheer total pleasure of it. I loved exploring roads which I had never driven before. I never tired of the boyish thrill of driving along country roads and zig-zagging along winding roads.

Driving along coastal roads, watching white horses galloping to shore carpeting the golden sands and looking skyward at cotton-ball clouds whipping across the almost blue summer sky—for me, this was one of life's unmistakable pleasures.

When I was driving, it was easy to forget about the worries of the day because I was so busy concentrating on the road and trying to predict what the other drivers might do.

It was a lovely, sunny spring morning as I drove to Inverness for one of my regular outings to the Highland capital. I enjoyed my outings to Inverness because it meant I could relax for a few hours away from the computer.

I tried to go on day outings to Inverness every month in the spring and summer as I enjoyed the drive. I loved gazing at the fields planted some months before, now showing signs of growth with winter barley.

As spring merged into summer, I loved seeing the yellow flowers of the rape seed oil plants swaying in the light breeze.

Driving downhill to Inverness, the view is incredible, with the Cromarty Firth on the right, and bottlenose dolphins leaping in the blue waters, and the Kessock Bridge in the distance with toy cars passing across it.

In the far distance I could see the white-cap peaks of the Black Isle and Ben Wyvis.

I knew that when I slowed to take the approaching left-hand bend (a turning on the right took you to Inverness Airport), I was only five miles from Inverness.

I turned left off the roundabout into the Retail Park, where I would reverse the car into one of the disabled bays and walk around to the back of the car to take my electric wheelchair out.

This was a safety measure on my part; if I fell backward, I would fall onto the path and not the road.

In later years and driving a new car, a VW Caddy, I was able to go from the driver's seat into my electric wheelchair and exit the vehicle via the back door by reversing down the ramp. The back door lifted automatically, and a ramp lowered by pressing a button on the key fob.

One day, I was using the lift to remove my electric wheelchair from the back of my Red Toyota Yaris Verso when I lost my footing and fell backward.

As I lay there on my back, I thought, *How am I going to get onto my knees?*

The general public are 99 percent very kind and helpful when you are a wheelchair user. Occasionally a member of the public does something that makes you say 'Wow' in amazement at their kindness.

One such incident happened to me that day. I was totally surprised by the lady's kind humility.

"Can I help you, sir?" the woman said in a caring voice full of concern.

I grunted an inaudible reply, and she said, "I was passing in the car and saw you lying on the ground, so I turned around to see if you needed help."

She helped me onto my knees, and from my knees I could use my car to hoist myself to a standing position.

I thanked the woman profusely, and she smiled and said she was glad to help. When she knew that I was safe, she went back to her car and went on about her day.

I will never forget the woman's kindness.

A total stranger, a fellow human being, going out of their way to help another human being in their time of need.

Kind acts like that illustrate to me that not everyone lives in their own self-absorbed world. Some people go out of their way to help others, and the planet is a better place for it.

Chapter 17

Summer Schools with the OU

As the years passed, my OU studies became more important to me. I had achieved the highest level of education offered by Moray College, and I was ready to advance my studies with the OU. I really enjoyed OU Summer Schools, which usually ran from Saturday to Saturday. The idea of these weeks is to give students experiences that go beyond what's taught in textbooks. For example, science students like me familiarised themselves with working in a laboratory and doing experiments. It was great fun!

I loved going to OU Summer Schools, but I hated getting to wherever the Summer Schools happened to be. Well, let me clarify that. It was great when the Summer School was in Scotland, and a couple of them were at Stirling University, and that was fantastic, but some of them were held at locations too far to drive to. That meant dealing with the maddening frustrations of public transport.

When you're a wheelchair user, public transport is a nightmare; that's been my experience anyway.

I was a biology student, so most of my Summer Schools were held at Nottingham University, though I did go to York University when I studied chemistry.

Driving that distance was too tiring and such a long way from the Northeast of Scotland.

Taking the train meant changes at different stations, and that meant even more hassles. When you're able to hop on a train, it's no problem, but it's a whole different ball game when you're in a wheelchair.

Buses are equally annoying, if not more of a hassle.

I flew to Nottingham as I thought it was less hassle and would get me there quicker. Less likely I would need the toilet on a short flight! Toilets and wheelchair access come high on my list of essential criteria.

When I arrived at the Summer School, I immediately loved the atmosphere as it was so electric and fun. The OU staff were all so welcoming and helpful.

I absolutely loved meeting students and learning about them and their experiences. I met some lovely people and made lasting friendships.

The OU is unique in that people who do different jobs, from QCs to refuse collectors, who might not meet in everyday life, come together with the common interest to advance their education.

Everyone is equal, and though they might have differing views on the same subject, their views have the same validity as anyone else's.

I cannot praise the OU highly enough for looking after their disabled students. No wonder the OU is the biggest educator of disabled people in the world. No one does it better!

At Summer Schools I got a mobility scooter and a helper. My helper stayed with me all week to get meals, open doors, and assist me in any way I needed.

The helpers were also OU students who gave up their time to volunteer to help fellow students. Lovely people.

I had two or three volunteers during my Summer Schools sessions. One of them I will never forget. Her name was Angela, and she was my helper when I attended a Summer School at Stirling University.

I had such a fun week, and Angela was a big part of my enjoyment. We laughed nearly all week. People knew we were coming down the hall before they saw us because of all the laughing we did!

Each day after the evening meal, the lecturers held optional tutorials for students to attend if they wanted. I wanted to attend one of the tutorials, but neither Angela nor I had been to the university before, so we didn't know our way about the place. Fellow students gave us directions on how to find the lecture theatre, but we were having so much fun talking and laughing that we completely got lost, which added to our laughter and fun.

I never did get to that tutorial!

I also recall, with a wry smile, another tutorial which I planned to attain, but never got there. I was studying one course and was going to visit a friend in central Scotland.

I wanted to attend this tutorial in Edinburgh and thought I could combine the two excursions: visit my friend and attend the tutorial.

That was the theory anyway, but it didn't go exactly to plan.

A lot of tutorials were around the central belt of Scotland because a lot of the OU tutors lived there.

A few were held in the North of Scotland at Culloden Academy (about fifty miles from where I lived in Fochabers), which I always enjoyed.

At last I could attend a tutorial without having to drive hundreds of miles.

Great! I thought.

I was staying at my friend's house for the weekend, and the tutorial was on Saturday morning. It started at 11:00 a.m. and would last about two hours.

Edinburgh was only thirty minutes or so from my friend's house.

Perfect!

"I'll be back for lunch," I said, leaning out of the driver's window.

Famous last words!

My friend gave me directions and waved me off.

"See you in a couple of hours," I called out through the open window.

I drove to Edinburgh without a problem and found the location where the tutorial was held, but I could not find the building. I got lost and drove around the city for hours.

I returned to my friend's house five hours later hungry and tired.

So much for lunch. Now it was time for supper!

Another time I attended a tutorial at Aberdeen College, about sixty miles away, and went for some lunch afterwards.

My car was locked inside the College's car park when I returned to get it a couple hours later. It took a lot of phone calling and waiting to get someone to show up with a key to unlock the gate!

Chapter 18

Doing My Bit

Over twenty plus years I volunteered with various charities and served in honorary positions from Chairman to Secretary. It was rewarding for the most part, but I always dreaded sitting through the meetings.

Nowadays I do not have to attend meetings, and my life is much better because of it!

There were comical moments over the years such as when I would turn up at the wrong venue and join the meeting in progress, and realise a while later that people were speaking about something completely different to what I thought they would be speaking about. That happened a few times.

Oops! Wrong meeting! I'd think to myself.

A couple of times I not only attended the wrong meeting but was at the wrong venue. How is it possible to mistake a different building?

Quite easily, I can assure you!

I went to one meeting, which I had attended once or twice before, but I hadn't paid close attention to the appearance of the building.

So, for this meeting, when I entered the building, I thought the place looked slightly different than before, but I didn't think more about it.

A while after the meeting had started, I began to notice things. *Hmm . . . the Chair doesn't look familiar. Neither does anyone else, come to that! In fact, I don't think I've been in this room before!*

Then I realised I was not only at the wrong meeting but in the wrong building.

Oh, dear! I thought. Sometimes I suffered in silence to the end of the meeting before making my apologies and hurrying to depart, but other times I scooted out mid-meeting because I couldn't bear the embarrassment and questioning looks!

Another thing that happened quite a lot with all the comings and goings was that I fell several times in car parks whilst walking around the car to stow my wheelchair in the boot, or the wheelchair would roll away as I leaned against the car to close the boot.

My party trick, nevertheless, was falling *under* the car.

One summer day whilst I was a trainer with Disability Equality Awareness Training (DEAT), I had finished a session at one of the local schools and had just stowed my wheelchair into the car's boot. I was walking around my car, holding on to the side panel, making my way to the driver's door when I lost my footing and slid along the length of the car.

As was typical of these falls, I was fully aware of what was going to happen next, and there was absolutely nothing I could do to lessen the impact.

Mary, the lady who organised DEAT, came out of a door to one of the buildings and saw me rolling about on the ground. Terrified that something was wrong, she shouted, "Are you alright, Iain?" as she came running over to help me.

I enjoyed my four or five years being a DEAT trainer.

Three of us were known as the Three Wise Monkeys: a man who was blind, a man who was deaf, and me, physically disabled due to Cerebral Palsy.

We were volunteers who gave up our time to help other people understand just a bit of what it was like to be disabled.

A lot of the local schools asked us to visit once a year or on a weekly basis. Private groups also asked us to give talks on disability awareness and accessibility.

Sometimes the teachers took a break from the classroom while I did my bit, and I was quite a dynamic character during my presentations. One of the teachers used to say, "I always know when you're here because of how much the kids are laughing!"

There's a whole generation who believe there are wheelchairs on the moon because of me!

The routines, mine anyway, were the same, but we all spoke without a script. In my opinion, this was essential, as we could react spontaneously to the kids' questions and interact with them naturally.

I have always had a silly sense of humour. When I was secretary for Shopmobility Moray from 1996 to 2011, Barbara, the coordinator, was often on the receiving end of my silliness and childish tricks.

One time I had a national radio station phone her at work, which threw her day off track, to put it mildly! And then there were all the computer pranks and other practical jokes I played on her.

Poor Barbara!

Barbara and I had a great working relationship. She was by far the cool-headed one.

I used to say, "You only need me to countersign cheques!"

Thank you, Barbara, for putting up with me all those years.

Chapter 19

My Life, My Way

In 2001 I moved into a Council house by myself in Fochabers. I moved in on Friday night, spent my first night in my new house, and was up early the next morning to attend an Open University tutorial at Inverness College.

Fochabers is a delightful village in the Northeast of Scotland. In the summer months the village looks beautiful with the blooming hanging baskets and containers bursting with flowers.

I loved Fochabers with all my heart like I have never loved any place before. I participated in village activities and spent money locally. I talked with everyone I met, and whenever I nipped to the shop, I enjoyed chatting with people along the way.

I soon became someone who was regularly seen around the village. Even while living in Fochabers I courted comical moments. I would do my shopping in the village, go back home, and be back ten minutes later because I had forgotten something, usually milk, and the assistants would say with big smiles as I entered the shop, "What have you forgotten this time?"

I loved wandering around the village exploring scenic walks. My favourite spot was looking down The Spey, a source of great solace, peace and tranquility.

I used to spend a lot of time at the Memorial Gardens gazing at The Spey flowing past. There is a bench on the grassy bank to invite people to sit and enjoy the view. I loved sitting next to it in my electric wheelchair. That bench inspired me to write the poem "The Seat" which you can find at the end of this book along with all of my poetry. I wondered one day how many people sat on that bench looking at the same view that I loved. On nice summer days, I enjoyed watching kayaks and canoes meandering down the river.

While nomadically zooming about the village, I was always thinking about my assignments and how to phrase essays or theses. When I was studying for my MSc (all those stress-free hours!), my itinerant lifestyle helped to focus my mind. Talking to people made the world a nicer place and washed the cares of the day away. I miss not having conversations with people in the village and visiting my usual places.

Happiness is often the simple things in life and cannot be replaced with coldness and sensibility, rationality and society's wrongly perceived ideas, not to mention the 'we know what's best for you' attitude uttered by those who should know better but often don't. Now, as I am embarking on my PhD, I will not have my beloved Fochabers to restore my calm tranquility and The Spey for academic inspiration. Whilst it is true that you can't eat scenery, as I have heard said, there's more to life than rational puritanism. Looking at calming scenery is good for us.

My house was perfect for my needs. There was a space for my car directly at the bottom of the ramp. The space was not on the road but was part of my house's property. It was at the front garden, but the Council built a ramp, and at the bottom of the ramp there was enough room for my car.

One early evening, I got out of the car and was about to walk up the ramp when I lost my balance and fell under the car.

About five minutes later, a neighbour who was out walking her dogs saw me lying there half under my car.

"Are you alright?" she said. "Is there anything wrong under the car?"

"No, everything's fine, thanks!" I said, and I proceeded to push myself onto my knees so I could use my elbow crutches to push myself into a standing position. By this point I was used to falling under my car, and I was a pro at righting myself. All in a day's work!

My house was high-tech in that I could operate things wherever I was in the house. This was mostly wonderful but sometimes frustrating. I wore an infrared control box around my neck that opened/closed the front door, switched on the lights, opened/closed the window blinds, and activated the community alarm in case I needed help.

I was always accidently activating the alarm, and a voice would eventually fill the room saying, "Is everything alright, Mr MacLeod?"

Worse still was when I mistakenly pressed the button after I'd had a shower, and the door to my house opened while I was walking to my bedroom naked!

I loved living in Fochabers and hoped I would end my days in the village. As with most things in life, things didn't go according to plan.

Chapter 20

Cherish Every Day

Thursday, 15th June, 2017, will be forever embedded in my brain as the day my life changed. I never could have imagined to what extent. The day started as every other day, but it would prove to be anything but an ordinary day. I would end the day lying in Intensive Care in an Aberdeen hospital with a ventilating tube down my throat.

I awoke at home that morning about the usual time, 6:00 a.m. The dawn chorus was singing merrily. I groped under the pillow to locate the controller that opens the door and blinds, turns on the lights, and switches on the TV and radio. Measuring about ten by five by three centimeters, I hung it around my neck with a black bootlace, turned down the duvet, and moved to get out of bed. Usually, I put on Radio Scotland each morning to find out the latest news, but for some strange reason, on that particular morning, I did not switch on the radio. Probably thought I would switch it on while sitting at the table having my first coffee of the day in about ten minutes.

A few months earlier, I had bought a memory foam mattress because the old mattress was sagging in the middle. On hindsight, it would prove to be the worst thing I ever bought. Rolling out of bed onto my knees that morning, which I did because the mattress was low to the floor, my left elbow slipped on the memory foam protector and wedged between the bed and the bedside cabinet. The morning before, my left hand slid off the mattress, and I had the passing thought, *I must remember to move that cabinet today.* I wish I had remembered! With my elbow wedged, I tried to heave my torso off the bed and onto the floor, but I did not have the strength. I lay strewn across the bed, right arm lying on the mattress at about one o'clock and the left arm wedged, palm against the cabinet and elbow against the side of the bed, my legs splayed open like pincers on the floor.

I was well and truly trapped.

I remember thinking, *How am I going to get out of this mess?*

The pain in my left arm was extremely severe, like no pain I had experienced before. I wriggled to free my arm, but it was jammed tight. Then, I had the bright idea to lower my wedged elbow down to the floor through the space between the cabinet and bed because that would allow me to get onto my knees and hoist myself to a standing position using my elbow crutches. Centimeter by centimeter, I worked my elbow down.

At this point, I actually thought my idea would work, but my elbow came to a sudden stop halfway down where the mattress meets the base of the bed and there were a few millimeters' gap. My bright idea did not work. In fact, it was going to prove an extremely bad idea. Instead of working its way loose, my elbow became more deeply lodged between the bed and the bedside cabinet.

Now I was well and truly trapped. Lying half sprawled across the mattress, half on the floor, I felt the fight for life slowly ebbing with every wriggle. The controller hung around my neck, but I could not reach it. I could not free myself.

Thinking back on that day, I might have had a small stroke as I lay trapped for eight hours, and this could have hampered my recovery.

I went to bed feeling fine and had an unbroken night's sleep just like the previous night and many nights before that.

I woke the next morning feeling fine and cannot contribute my accident to feeling unwell.

I got out of my bed the same way I had done every morning since moving to Fochabers some seventeen years before. Why getting out of bed that morning went so horribly wrong, and not on previous mornings, I do not know.

Getting up that morning did go wrong, and now I must live my life as a severely disabled person. I have lost my cherished independence and am unable to do anything for myself physically. I must rely on carers to look after me. I cannot drive anymore, and that is the hardest pill I've had to swallow, as I loved driving and foolishly thought I would always be able to drive.

It is natural to think *if only*... but life is full of 'if only' moments, and nothing will ever change the fact that I cannot do as much for myself now as I could before.

This is the here and now, and whether I like it or not, that's how things are.

I must play the hand I'm dealt.

That is exactly what I have decided to not sit around wallowing in self-pity. It is much better to carry on being ambitious and achieving things.

My brainpower has not been affected in any way. I am still as sharp thinking as I ever was, probably even sharper.

Boy, that's scary!

I did not suddenly become academic overnight. It took years of dedication and commitment, and I am not going to sit back and do nothing just because I need help with the mundane tasks of daily living. Who doesn't want a little help with those anyway?!

My dream of earning a doctorate degree is going to happen. That's a no-brainer as far as I am concerned. My accident has robbed me of many things, but ambition and pushing the boundaries are not amongst them. I have not lost any of my sheer determination to accomplish what I set my mind to.

Sit back and watch others achieve things while I do nothing? Not a chance! I am here to make my mark in the world as long as I have breath in my body. Becoming a published author is yet another notch, and I also hope to motivate and inspire my readers to set the bar high for themselves too, no matter their ability or disability.

I want to encourage parents of children with Cerebral Palsy or other disabilities to let them experience as much as possible.

Do not be afraid to let them live their own life.

Don't wrap them in cotton wool!

They will make mistakes as everyone does.

I certainly made mistakes, but I matured and became a better man for it. I experienced the boost in self-confidence that comes from royally screwing up and figuring a way out of the mess I'd made!

It will be hard to let them fend for themselves and to watch them make mistakes, but they will thank you for it in the long run.

My parents allowed me to experience many things in my life, and for that I am truly thankful to them. It must have been so hard on my parents, especially my Mum, to watch me drive off to live by myself that September evening in 2001.

They soon realised that I could manage on my own, and I was ready to live life my way in my new environment in my own home.

On that note, I would love to live in my own specially designed smart house someday.

I have learned new skills since my accident in 2017, and I've grown in ways that I never even considered before.

One of my biggest accomplishments? I am now a published author. My first book, *10 seconds That Changed My Life*, tells the story of the morning of my accident and my thirteen-month journey through four hospitals.

I encourage you to read it to discover that no matter how tough life gets, and for me it seemed to have gone from bad to worse, there is indeed light at the end of the tunnel, and you must strive on no matter how hard it might seem at the time.

Cherish each day and live it to the fullest extent possible. Every moment is precious, and not to be wasted. Life is for living, not waiting to live. You can do more than you ever dreamed possible. I believe in you!

A Note from the Author

I have lived in a sheltered housing complex in Elgin since July 2018. It is a beautiful place to stay, and the carers are all good, lovely people.

Broadband is fantastic, and it enables me to do virtually everything online from my academic studies to writing books to ordering groceries.

Being a bit of a tech-head, I use technology to make my life easier. I use voice recognition devices to keep me entertained and to switch on the lights.

I need a lot of care, and all the carers are so kind and we have a good laugh. Because I rely on the carers to do everything for me, we have a special relationship. I trust them empirically.

Of course, I find the whole situation strange at times—having others look after me, especially since I cherished my independence so much and assumed, like most people do, that I would always be able to look after myself.

Life is unpredictable at the best of times. You never know what's around the corner. You learn to adapt, and what might have seemed strange becomes your new normal.

Over the passage of time I have found an inner tranquility and acceptance of my new reality. I understand that others must look after me instead of me looking after myself.

Admitting to yourself that you need more help than would normally be the case is the first step toward living your life to the full.

Life is what you make of it, and I have become more appreciative of my immediate surroundings.

For fifty-three years, I lived life in the fast lane, but now I've had to slow down. The work still gets done, and I am less tired and find enormous satisfaction in talking to my good friend Ron who lives in my housing complex. Coincidentally, Ron and I spent six months in two hospitals together and have a special bond as result. He's a former fireman, and we have certainly been through the fire together and lived to tell about it.

Life is good!

Iain M. MacLeod
wheelsgalore100@gmail.com
https://www.wheelsgalore.scot

Poetic Musings on Life, Ability, and My Beloved Scotland

Stornoway Gael

Madainn mhath and Feasgar math
Gaelic phrases of my youth
In a land of ancient tradition and cleared people
Sheep over people

I lie in the sofa bed, in a Laxdale living room,
watching the magenta skyline
Watching, through the four paneled windows,
the sodium silhouette of Stornoway
Land of my nostalgic reminiscences and pride
Berthed Cullivan ready to return to Ullapool
Right lies Stornoway Castle standing guard over the island

Laxdale, a few miles north of Stornoway
Up the cluthan and to the right
Tar roofed white cottage with lovingly crafted peat stack

Long days cutting peats at Loch Crinabhat
Eaten alive by midges
Tea made from ice-cold well water, best ever
Crackan biscuits, hard insides and brown outer
Superbly delicious with butter and jam
An anticipated treat

Recollections of a bygone age
Brown corrugated cowshed at the bottom of the croft
Once a sanctuary of bovine activity
Now a refuse for feral kittens

Walking down the starran for adventures
Green wire-messed gate; end of a stony dirt track
Protection from the outside world

Running down the croft
Before becoming a member of the lifelong club
Asian flu robbing a boy of his childhood and adulthood

Instead succumbing to societal vagaries
Relatives reminding of this loss
"I remember when...!" only served to frustrate
Early years of forgotten blankness

Now, on the downward spiral, a time to reflect
Long summers of distant memories
Rose tinted views of idealism and utopian perfection
Though it might not have been
The desire to go back to Stornoway does not appeal
Reminiscences are historical recollections of the past
Always will be proud of being a Gael and of my heritage

Callanish Stones

A land shrouded in mystical and ancient past
People worshipped celestial gods
Offerings of appeasement ritually offered
To improve body or receive spiritual forgiveness

Callias respectful of their ancient inhabitants
Stone circle in praise of astronomical wonderment
The village courteously gracious of centuries past
Their achievements and pious reverence worshipped

Stones of past civilisation erected in homage
Their mystical significance remains lost in time
Ancestral ancestors impregnate my DNA
My time capsule to the past lies biologically hidden
The lineage will end with me

Distant Hills

Scotland's hills of towering majestic magnificence
Bring memories of wonderment and magnitude
Deceptively deceiving in their imposing splendour

Glencoe magnetically draws the brave and foolhardy
Osmotically drinking the atmosphere with every breath
Captivated with their impressive grandeur
Buachaille Etive Beag and Bidean nam Bian
Meal Dearg and Sgorr nam
Fiannaidh and Sgorr Dhearg and Sgorr Dhonuill
Guardians of secrets of a massacre century past

Climbers climb being mesmerised by beauty
Some triumph and some do not
And remain encapsulated in a world without end
Hills of tranquility and seductive elegance
Attractive appeal and deceiving deception
Geology often overcomes biological endeavours

Old Schoolyard

Boarded up the stone building weathers
Not revealing past years of educational achievements
People who stop unaware of childhood dreams
Abandoned and vacant and neglected
Unknowing testament of a forgotten past

Children played and laughed together and loved
Not caring of the world and its introspective harshness
Unaware of life's multiplicity of layered carpeting
Labelled chained boxes of physical imperfections
Lifelong barriers to overcome of unfilled aspirations
Those were the days of untarnished minds
Unconcerned and carefree childhoods
Unknowing of the world that lay beyond
Unconscious of what the future may hold
How the labelled boxes would shape and determine.

Days of uncluttered purity and innocent childhood
Distant remembrances in a sterile environment
Decades pass, memories become transient
Old adages of imbecilic slowly diminishing
Memories fade as downward slope looms
Old school yard gradually fades in the mists of time

PMR

Princess Margaret Rose Hospital, restorer of life
Princess Margaret Rose, daughter of King George
IV Southside of Edinburgh
The seriously ill child lay helpless and dying
Asian flu assigning the child to the lifelong club
Succumbing to societal vagaries and patronisation
Life's badge for being different in a perfect world

Slowly and painfully, he recovered
Endured operation after operation
Body crafted and molded to semi-perfection
Mr. Fulford rebuilt and crafted and restored
Surgical skill artistry shaped the sculpture

Life's path divided and the one less travelled trundled
Swaying from side to side, the turns undulated
A world of stereotype nothing objects
Educated to below par was the 'normal' expectation
Overcoming hurdles proved to be a lifetime occupation
Perceived normality was never an option
In a world of perfection and flawless purities
The downward spiral question's the point of life

Patronising Perceptions

The figure sits in his own small world
Bereft of sense and rationality and neuronal connections
How graciously society bestows accolades

Readily the crown of physical imperfections honoured
Broca's damage just adds to the imbecilic patronising
Retardation and disability is causally linked insinuated
Educated to just write their names
"After all, that's all they will need," the 'professionals' procrastinate
Preaching Freudian misguided nonsense
In a world of psychological bombastic bureaucrats
The old school mentality continues in ridiculousness

The figure sits thinking of his thesis and possibilities
Lost in his own world of higher educational attainment
Higher than the procrastinating professionals
Who want to take the praise and credit
Personal endeavour and fulfilment the only driving force

Sanctimonious Hypocrisy

Geocentrically orbiting the Earth rotationally
Milky Way of infinite empty space
Revolving ball of humanity and caring sanctuary

A World of self-righteous duplicity and perfection
Hypocritical flawless impurities and puritanism
The latest teabag or the unseasonality of the weather
Designed to show the simplicity of character

Subliminal Darwinism is purposely disguised
Survival of the fittest ensures differentiation continues
Denial rigorously refuted with epitaph proportionality

The world continues to spin on its axis
Caring do-gooders continue to speak new teabags

Simplistic patronisation judged on Brocial appearance
Spontaneity will never be without character familiarity
Species propagation potentially and superiority

Fochabers

Driving away that Friday night heralded a new chapter
Late September weather transition merged
Friday night Fochabers, Saturday Inverness

Not realising the empathetic pull of the village
Bonds deepen over the rolling years

House crafted and tailored to suit
Doors marked are characteristics of hidden happiness
Satisfaction of ecstasy a gauge of blissful contentment
Contented dwelling is testament of pride and fulfilment
Unconscious realisation of singleton reality

Wheeled freedom represents solitude tranquility
Aimlessly chaired wandering naturally rejuvenates
Physical barriers of normal chains are briefly broken

The northeast village unaware of personal happiness
Spinning striped recognition being inner contentment
In a world of uncertainty and insecurity
Fochabers restores clarity and peaceful satisfaction

The Spey a source of great joyous pleasure
Looking down the undulating waters of restoration
Calming qualities of tranquility soothingly washes
In an act of contemplative meditation
A neural confusion to placid peacefulness

Autumn Colours

Crimson reds and oranges and rustic browns and
lemony yellow interspersed in a lime canopy
A wall of multi-coloured leaves
A waterfall of hued descending leaves

Multi-coloured branches
Guardians of remembrance stones of loved ones departed
Overlooking the Spey
Reassurance of the flowing waters
White horses cascading to form swirls

Water glints in autumn sun
Falling from the sky like leaves falling from trees
Blanketed soil in readiness for next spring's birth

Belly Clock

Standing guard with reassuring presence since 1798
On the hour every hour the time booms out
Reverberating near and far
Performing a valuable information service

Steadfastly booming out its hourly prompt
Reminder of an appointment or catching a bus
Timekeeping for activities of daily importance
Or just a gentle reminder of the hours passing

The clock is a focal feature of daily life
Witness to triumph and sadness
A bystander to days of wedding celebrations

Sad departing souls of the great and good
Every facet of village life throughout the years

Fountain Focality

Commemorating water to Fochabers in 1798
The fountain is a prominent feature
Focal point for all to see and admire
Obvious treasure for locals and tourists alike
Sitting transfixed in wonderment
Whiling the time away in mesmerising tranquility
A landmark and point of reference for placement

A conspicuous symbiotic marriage with the clock
Standing guard over the village in an angel-like way
Cascading water symbolises cleansing from high
Architectural details of past craftsmanship is a legacy
Five cherubs make sure all is well as guardian angels

Commemoration has become guardianship
For all to see and admire adoringly in forbearance
Lasting inheritance of remembrance from the past

Buzzing Bonanza

The bee methodically circles, buzzing from plant to plant
A ritualistic dance passed down the generations
Orbiting the flowers with precision probing
Gathering the sweet nectar for storage

Focused on the task it was born
Single-minded unwavering

Concentrating on its mission
Obtaining nutritious nectar for the next generation

Next generation methodically circles
The genetic cycle of probing passes to the next

The Wind

Ripples of icy cold water swirls down the Spey
In an act of abeyance to the howling December wind
Bowing respectfully to its master's superiority
Its preponderance ascendancy and pre-eminence

Bone-chillingly cold yet strangely invigorating
The glacial rawness of the wind in your face
Eyes smarting and nose constantly running
Blasts of the Northerly on your cheeks
Arctic piercing chill penetrating through the layers
Cocooned in duck-down or synthetic compounds

The cold icy wind blows down the Spey
Little sign of life in the water or on the banks
Looking down the flowing watery wintery scene
Distant landscape lies barrow and bleak and cold
The Shortest Day herald's balmy summery warmth.

Lady with the Mystic Smile

People move to the side, parting the waves
Shuffles to leave a clear passage
'Let the wheelchair through,' security said

Symbol of recognisable difference
A chariot; unknowing announcement and simplicity

Da Vinci's *Mona Lisa* still draws magnetically
Osmotically drinking in the
Lady's smile and charisma
Shrouded mystery of her true identity fascinates
Who is she? What was the connection?
Centuries roll and theories mount, but no definitive
A series of possibilities adds to the conundrum

The Louvre, right of the Seine, home to *Mona Lisa*
How far removed from Italy and her lifestyle
Now being spied upon in a conspicuous capital
Solitary hanging for all to admire and marvel
Small in presence though tall in popular recognition
Eyes; following in an act of compulsive observation

Japanese Acer

Shrouded in oriental mystical past
Mountain maple grows uninhibited skyward
Looking elegant covered in a deep red bark

The cold frosty days of winter the Acer illuminates
Joyously lighting up the long dreary days
In an act of steadfastly urban sophistication

Symbiosis from the other plants seems to encourage
Prompting and supporting and inspiring
Allied champion of other forms of nature to survive

Birds shelter and rest and forage for sustaining food
Insects single-mindedly scurry on their life cycle

From my window I watch the seasonal changes
Spring heralds rebirth of buds and nutritional growth
Summer sees an efflorescence array of bloom
Autumn the windswept cascading waterfall of leaves
Winter bareness in readiness to start the cycle again

The Spey

Majestic sounds of the water flowing past
Streaming over rocks in a fluidity of forcefulness
Salmon leaping on their migratory journey
Canoes weave their way to their destination

I sit in reflective solitude
My beloved Spey soothes and washes and cleanses
Picturesque vistas and flowing, restores neural calmness
The waters inspire as well as rejuvenate
Neural synaptic connections intertwine galvanised thought processes

My beloved Spey swirls and surges on its journey unaware of its
comforting tranquility

The Seat

Picture framed between trees
Overlooking the Spey as it flows past
Rod fishing for salmon forms the migratory dance
Canoes weaving their way eastward

The seat is witness to all habitation of the Spey
Exposed to all the elements from baking heat to snow
Patiently waiting for its next passing viewer to sit

Generations finding solitude and comfort
Retired GPs to Londoners seeking Scottish romance
All searching for inner peace
All lost in contemplative pondering
Admiring the picturesque scenes

Mind drifting and reflecting
Troubles being washed and purified
Amidst the uninterrupted continuous water
Reflecting on life's strangeness and tragic woes
Finding calm and peace and inner tranquility

Glassic-Gibbon wrote, "The land endures..."
And the seat endures
Restoring rationality and peacefulness
Unknowingly the river surges past on its journey
Unaware of its rejuvenating harmonious serenity

Open University

Educator of the masses without societal barriers
All coming together in a common unity
Society's class statuses hold no governing rule
Instead passion and enthusiasm and eagerness
Advancement and achievement and pride objectives
Giving hope to the dejected and dreams to dreamers
In a voyage of discovery to explore unforeseen worlds

The OU largest educator of disabled
Societal barriers of preconceptions
Imbecilic condescending supercilious chains are broken

My beloved OU is there in dark and joyous times
Non-judgmental of physical imperfections

Neural achievements are the only criteria
A constant when life becomes overbearing
Access with no barriers and an addicted student
True equality and not just meaningless sound bites

Opportunity of sameness is refreshing in its parity
No diminishing of educational standards
Same TMAs and EMAs exasperated expectations
Same frustrating neural stress and pleasurable thrill
Equality at its finest with no barriers

In a world of uncertainty and fakery
The OU is a shining light to show the way
Few can follow the leader though try but fail
Educator of the masses and destroyer of myths
Restoring confidence and hope to ultimate success